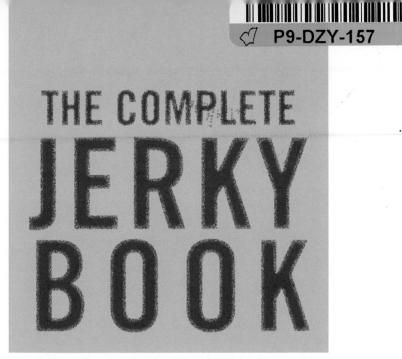

THE COMPLETE JERKY BOOK

HOW TO DRY, CURE, AND PRESERVE EVERYTHING FROM VENISON TO TURKEY

MONTE BURCH

Skyhorse Publishing

Skyhorse Publishing books may be purchased in bulk at special discounts for sales promotion, corporate gifts, fund-raising, or educational purposes. Special editions can also be created to specifications. For details, contact the Special Sales Department, Skyhorse Publishing, 307 West 36th Street, 11th Floor, New York, NY 10018 or info@skyhorsepublishing.com.

Skyhorse® and Skyhorse Publishing® are registered trademarks of Skyhorse Publishing, Inc.®, a Delaware corporation.

Visit our website at www.skyhorsepublishing.com.
www.skyhorsepublishing.com

20 19 18 17 16 15 14 13 12 11

Library of Congress Cataloging-in-Publication Data

Burch, Monte.
  The complete jerky book : how to dry, cure, and preserve everything from venison to turkey / Monte Burch.
      p. cm.
  ISBN 978-1-61608-040-2 (pbk. : alk. paper)
  1. Dried beef. 2. Dried meat. 3. Cookery (Game) I. Title.
  TX749.5.B43B79 2010
  641.6'6–dc22

                                        2010008172

Printed in China

Contents

Introduction

I've hunted deer from Alaska to Mexico and just about everywhere in between, and one thing I've noticed is that, no matter where you are, you can always count on someone bringing jerky to deer camp. Hunting camp wouldn't be the same without it.

I don't know how many deer I've taken over the years, but a great deal of my venison has gone into jerky. Our family has been making and snacking on jerky since the early 1970s. Even today, there's usually a jar of it on my office desk, at least until my supply runs out. When I'm out hunting, I always have some while I'm sitting in my tree stand, waiting for a whitetail to come by. Jerky is a great snack, and it can be made out of just about any lean meat, including domestic meats. Beef is the most common meat for commercially made jerky, while homemade jerky can made from all different kinds of wild game.

In days past, jerky making was an essential survival skill; today it's more of a hobby, a great way to utilize venison or other meat, and provide a tasty, nutritious snack food. Jerky making can be as simple as slicing meat into thin strips and drying, or can be more involved by grinding and adding any number of spices. It's a fun pastime, especially when you start experimenting with different recipes. Making jerky is a great way to learn an ancient skill, and will provide you with an appreciation of the ways of our ancestors. In this book, you'll find the oldest and the latest information on making jerky. You'll find many old and new recipes, some resurrected from the past, some taken from my family's recipe books, and others garnered from friends and deer-camp buddies who all enjoy making jerky. We hope you'll enjoy this enough to start making jerky own your own. Just be forewarned: Once you become involved in this fun and rewarding hobby, you'll be hooked for a long time.

—Monte Burch, Humansville, MO, February 2010

CHAPTER

All About Jerky

The word "jerky" is derived from a Peruvian term, *quichua* (pronounced kee-chew-a). The native South American Quechua term, *ch'arki* or *charque,* came from this, and means "dried meat." The term eventually made its way north and was adopted by Native Americans. Early scouts, explorers, and trappers heard the word and soon turned it into "jerky."

While we can trace the origins of the word, no one really knows how the ancient process of drying meat for storage began. The technique of drying meat, fruits, and vegetables to preserve them is one of mankind's oldest skills. You wonder who actually discovered that a hunk of mastodon meat left in the sun was still edible, and began the process. Dried meat not only does not decay or invite insect infestation as much as fresh meat, but it can be stored for periods of time and is lightweight, making it easy to transport and eat on the go—the original fast food. This was extremely important for hunters and gatherers as they often killed game and foraged far from their campsites, consuming the dried meat as they followed future food sources.

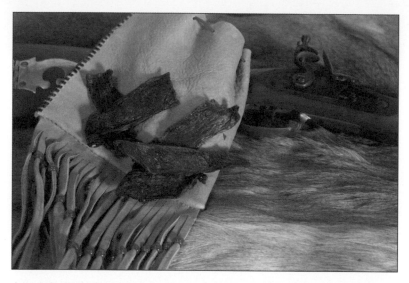

A staple food since mankind's beginnings, jerky was a common food of the Native Americans and was carried by the explorers, trappers, and scouts as they discovered and opened North America.

No longer a staple in some modern cultures, today jerky is primarily a snack food—an extremely nutritious food that you can take outdoors or enjoy at home.

There is evidence that jerky was produced thousands of years ago in ancient Egypt. It became an important food back then because it could be produced in large quantities and stored, adding to the diet of dried grain that most people ate. Jerky was introduced into Europe in the 1500s by the Spaniards who then, during the early conquest of the Americas, brought their jerky into North America. Native Americans, including the Inuits, were already well versed in drying game meats and fish. As the North American continent was explored, jerky became a staple and much valued food source. Trappers, traders, and explorers lived off jerky as they made their way across the continent. Today jerky is not considered a staple food, but rather, a popular and nutritious snack food.

BENEFITS

Dried meat is very dense and provides a concentrated source of nutrients. Jerky, which is made from lean meat, is low in fat and cholesterol and high in protein and energy. A pound of meat will weigh about 4 ounces after it has been made into jerky. With most of the moisture removed, jerky is more shelf stable and can be stored without refrigeration for short periods of time. Because of that, jerky is a favorite food of backpackers, hunters, fishermen, and outdoorsmen.

Just about any type of meat can be dried, including meat from game animals such as deer, moose, and elk; domestic livestock such as cows and pigs; and birds or fowl, including game birds such as turkeys, pheasants, ducks, and geese. Fish have also traditionally been dried for storage. Fruit such as apples can even be dried into jerky-like strips, although these are called leather, not jerky. One of the most commonly used meats is venison. If you have a successful deer season, you may have more venison than you want to cook normally, and jerky is an excellent way of preserving the lesser cuts, especially if the meat is made into ground jerky. If you wish to put the entire deer into jerky, a white-tailed deer that weighs 150 pounds will typically field dress to about 115 to 120 pounds. This will yield about 75 to 80 pounds of meat. If you make all of the meat into jerky, you should have between 15 and 20 pounds of jerky.

Making your own jerky is easy, fun, and a great way of preserving and utilizing meat from game animals such as white-tailed deer.

TODAY'S METHODS

Jerky was once made by simply hanging strips of meat over a tree limb. This resulted in a product that was very tough and long lasting. Today's jerky can be made under more controlled conditions, providing a much softer and tastier food. Like wine or beer making, jerky making is part science and part art. It's fun to experiment with different recipes.

Jerky can be made using several methods, including slicing the meat to produce muscle-meat jerky and grinding it to produce ground jerky. Ground meat is shaped into thin strips or sticks.

The simplest way to make jerky is to slice muscle meat into strips to be dried. These strips can be cured by adding a dry mix, which is rubbed into and mixed with the meat, or by allowing the strips to marinate in a liquid cure. A more modern method involves grinding the meat, mixing it with cure and spices, extruding or rolling the meat flat, and cutting it into strips.

READY-MADE JERKY

Commercially made jerky is also widely available in several forms. "Beef jerky," for example, is made from a single piece of beef. "Beef jerky, chunked and formed," is made from chunks of meat that are molded and formed, then cut into strips. "Beef jerky ground and formed or chopped and formed" is produced from meat that is ground or chopped, then molded and cut into strips. Beef jerky containing binders or extenders must name the added ingredient or ingredients in the product's name, such as "beef and soy protein concentrate jerky, ground and formed." "Jerky sausage" consists of meat that has been chopped and stuffed, then dried into casings.

Commercially produced jerky, most commonly made from beef, is a popular and nutritious snack food.

Tools and Materials

KNIVES

A sharp knife is the only tool you really need to create jerky. Merely slice the meat into strips and hang over tree branches or build a hanging rack from sprouts and saplings (if the temperature and weather conditions are right). Having more than one knife makes the task easier, though. The ultimate is to have a number of knives on hand in a variety of shapes for the many different chores.

If you field dress and skin big game, a skinning knife with a fairly short blade and a gut hook makes the job much easier. The blade shape should be rounded and with a drop point so you can slice the skin from the muscle without cutting the skin. The same fairly short knife can also be used for cutting up the meat during the butchering process, but regular butcher knives, with longer blades, are best for this chore.

I inherited a number of old-time butcher knives, including some that were actually carried by trappers and explorers, and I

Actually, only one tool is needed for making jerky—a sharp knife.

still enjoy using them. Butcher knives come in a wide variety of sizes and shapes, and again, different types are used for different chores. Wide-bladed knives are best for slicing meat into thin strips to create jerky or chunks to grind into ground jerky. Thin-bladed, more flexible knives are best when deboning meat for jerky. I actually prefer the rounded-tip butcher knives over those with a sharp tip for cutting meat into smaller pieces, because the upswept tip doesn't catch on meat as you slice it. You can also buy butcher knife sets with a variety of knife shapes included. Some sets even include a sharpening steel. The RedHead Deluxe Butcher Knife Kit, for example, includes a paring knife, boning knife, butcher knife, meat cleaver, spring shears, square tube saw, honing steel, cutting board, butcher's apron, and six pairs of gloves—all in one case.

Always buy and use quality knives. Not only are they easier to use, but they are safer because they will keep an edge longer and

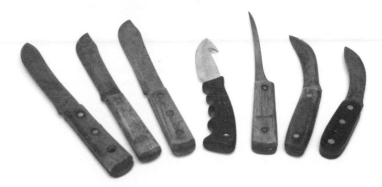

If you have a variety of knives, you'll be able to pick the right one for each specific chore. From left to right are butcher knives, a hunting knife with gut hook for field dressing, a thin-bladed boning knife, and two old-time skinning knives.

(Photo courtesy Bass Pro Shops)

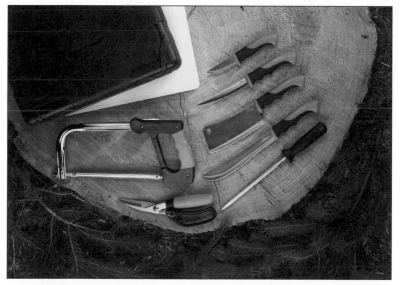

This RedHead Deluxe Butcher Kit has a selection of knives suited to the specific butchering chores, as well a meat cleaver, meat saw, and sharpening steel.

are easier to sharpen. When purchasing a new knife, the blade should have a sharp edge and should resist dulling, but it should also be easy to sharpen. A variety of handle shapes and materials are also used in knife construction. In quality knives, the handles will be made most commonly of hardwood or a synthetic material. The latter, sometimes comprised of soft-molded materials, are easy on the hands for long periods of use.

In addition to having a variety of quality knives, it's important to understand the types of steel used in knives. Knife blades are made of three different types of steel: carbon, stainless steel, and high-carbon stainless steel. Carbon was the original steel used in knife construction, and many old carbon-steel knives are still in use, including several in my collection. Carbon steel is relatively soft and sharpens very easily, even with nothing more than a hand-held stone. On the other hand, it doesn't hold an edge very well and must be continually sharpened. Carbon steel also rusts badly, even if the metal is dried after cleaning. One solution is to lightly spray the metal with cooking oil before storage. Always wash the knife thoroughly before reusing to remove any residual oil and/or rust. Pure stainless steel is the hardest of the three metals, but it's almost impossible to sharpen correctly at home. Stainless steel will, however, hold an edge almost forever once sharpened, and it does not rust. The majority of the knife blades today are made from high-carbon stainless steel. This material provides the best of both worlds: a fairly easily sharpened blade that will hold an edge for a reasonable time and doesn't rust as badly as carbon steel.

Knife blade edges are commonly ground into one of three shapes: flat ground, hollow ground, or taper ground. Flat-ground blades have their edge ground evenly from the back of the blade to the front of the blade and from the heel to the point. These blades are sturdy and easily sharpened. Hollow-ground edges have a thinned portion of the blade just behind the edge. This creates less drag, but it also creates a weak area in the blade. A better solution is a taper-ground knife, whereby an additional grind is made after the flat grind to thin out the blade without the thinness of a hollow-ground edge. A taper ground produces a knife with little drag but more strength than a hollow-ground edge, and it's only found on high-quality knives.

SHARPENING

Keeping knife blades sharp is an extremely important facet of any type of meat preparation. Using the proper tools can make it easy to have sharp knives as needed. A wide variety of knife-sharpening devices are available, ranging from the simple but extremely effective butcher's steel to powered sharpeners. Knives in good shape, but dull, should never be sharpened with a powered grinder, as

(B & C Photos courtesy Chef'sChoice)

It's extremely important to keep knives sharp. A variety of sharpening devices are available. I've used Chef's Choice power sharpeners and hones for a number of years now. They're extremely efficient and produce razor-sharp edges in seconds. Shown are the 120, 220, and 1520 models.

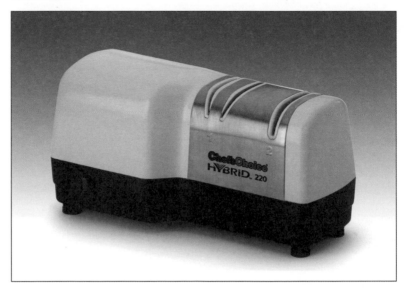

you stand a good chance of overheating the steel and losing the temper. Powered sharpening hones, however, can make the chore of sharpening a dull knife quick and easy. I've used Chef'sChoice models for many years, and I particularly like the Chef'sChoice Professional Model 130. It will sharpen both straight and serrated edges and has a 125-watt motor with three sharpening stages: a 40-degree pre-sharpening, a 45-degree sharpening, and a third steeling stage for final sharpening. Springs guide the blade for precise sharpening. The Model 120 has similar features, except a stropping stage replaces the steeling stage for a Trizor® triple bevel edge. The Chef'sChoice Diamond Hone AngleSelect Sharpener, Model 1520, is engineered to put a razor-sharp edge on all quality

(Photo courtesy Bass Pro Shops)

One of the best hand-sharpening units I've used is the Lansky Sharpening System. The system is available in three different kits that consist of hone holders that are color coded for easy identification of the exact sharpening angles desired.

Keep an old-fashioned butcher steel close at hand for regularly retouching the blades of knives as you use them.

Another sharpener to keep on the butcher table is the Lansky hand sharpener. A hand guard protects your hand.

knives, and it can restore and recreate both a 20-degree edge for European- and American-style knives and a 15-degree edge for Asian-style knives. The multi-beveled, razor-sharp, 15-degree edge on hunting knives reduces the amount of effort needed to cut or fillet, making it ideal for skinning and field dressing. A more economical sharpener is the Chef'sChoice Hybrid Sharpener. The Hybrid technology combines electric and manual sharpening and features two stages: an electric–powered stage for sharpening and a manual stage for honing. The Hybrid 220 couples the two stages with precise bevel angle control to provide a super-sharp, arch-shaped edge that is stronger and more durable than the conventional V-shaped or hollow-ground edges.

Another system I've found extremely effective and easy to use is the Lansky Sharpening System. The kit contains finger-grooved hone holders that are color coded for easy identification of the exact sharpening angles desired. Knife clamp with angle selector, guide rods, extra attachment screws, oil, and a sharpening guide all come in a handy carrying case. Three kits are available. The Standard Kit has coarse, medium, and fine hones; the Deluxe Kit has extra-coarse, coarse, medium, fine, and ultra-fine hones; and the Diamond Kit has coarse, medium, and fine diamond hones.

An old-fashioned butcher's steel is actually the quickest and easiest tool for keeping an edge on blades as you work. Simply draw the blade across the steel a couple of times if it starts to dull between cuts. Another extremely simple and efficient sharpener for at-hand work is the Lansky Hand Sharpener. You'll want to keep either of these tools close at hand for quick, touch-up sharpening.

WORK TABLE

In addition to knives, a wide range of tools can enhance the ease, speed, and safety of making jerky. Next to a knife, the most important piece of equipment is a good, solid working table or surface that can be easily cleaned. Your kitchen table or kitchen countertop will work, but it should not be wood or even the traditional butcher block. Rather, it should be an easily cleaned, non-porous surface. A number of years ago, I bought a pair of stainless-steel tables at a school auction. These are ideal, as they can be cleaned and sanitized without much effort. Restaurants that are going out

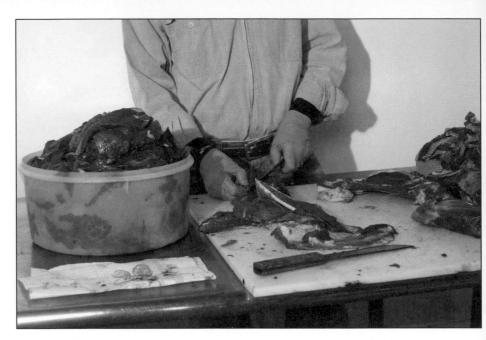

You'll need a quick-to-clean, nonporous work surface. An easily cleanable table, such as the second-hand, stainless-steel table shown, is ideal. You can also use a large synthetic cutting board.

of business will often have these for sale as well. In lieu of the ultimate table, a large synthetic cutting board is the next best option.

SLICERS

For sliced muscle-meat jerky, the Hi Mountain Jerky Board and Knife Kit makes slicing jerky to thicknesses of ⅛ or ¼ of an inch quick and easy to do with precision. The kit contains a cutting board with a holding lip around each side to cut both ⅛- and ¼-inch-thick slices. Lay the meat in place, hold it down securely, and use the

The Hi Mountain Jerky Board and Knife kit makes it easy to cut precise thicknesses of meat for muscle-meat jerky. The kit includes selected jerky seasonings for a quick start at producing your own sliced jerky.

Slicing meat is faster and easier with an electric slicer, and you can slice precise thicknesses. I've been using Chef'sChoice slicers for many years. Their Model 650 is a folding slicer that you can store easily or take to your hunting cabin.

The Chef'sChoice VariTilt electric slicer is a professional model with a heavy duty motor and is capable of tilting for gravity slicing.

included stainless-steel slicing knife to cut the strips to the desired thickness. The kit also comes with selected jerky seasonings.

Of course, the ideal for slicing a large amount of muscle meat into jerky is an electric slicer such as the Chef'sChoice models. Again, I've used a number of these products over the years. Their Model 650 is a great little slicer that will fold down to three inches and pack easily to slice even in camp. The Chef'sChoice Model 645 VariTilt is a higher grade, with a 130-watt condenser motor, and can slice from extremely thin-shaved slices to slices as thick as you desire.

GRINDERS

Using ground meat to make jerky has become increasingly popular. The resulting jerky is not as tough as muscle-meat jerky, can make use of less choice meat cuts and meat trimmings, and can be seasoned with a wide range of flavorings. However, ground meat jerky will require a meat grinder. If you're only doing a small amount of jerky, a hand-grinder may be your best choice. These are economical and easy to use. Of course, they are only as fast as you can hand-crank them, and they do require muscle power. This heavy-duty bolt-on model grinds 5 to 6 pounds per minute and comes with ⅜- and ³⁄₁₆-inch plates, grinding knife, and sausage stuffing tube. For many years I used a large antique grinder I inherited from my grandfather. It had a big flywheel and was powered by a big electric motor with a belt. My granddad originally powered the grinder with his Model-A, jacking up the rear wheels and running the grinder with a big belt.

(Photos courtesy Bass Pro Shops)

Ground meat jerky is extremely popular for many reasons, and it's relatively easy to produce. Ground meat will require a grinder. Small amounts of jerky can be run through a hand grinder. Hand grinders are available as clamp-on or bolt-on models.

An electric grinder speeds up the work and makes the chore of grinding meat easier. If electricity is available where you grind, anyone who grinds much game meat or meat for ground jerky will sooner or later have an electric grinder. Look for grinders that are sturdy, have easy-to-clean parts of stainless steel, and are also easy to use. The No. 12 Model shown here grinds 360 pounds of meat per hour.

The ultimate is a powered grinder, and they're available in a number of sizes depending on the horsepower, which determines the amount of meat that can be ground in an hour. Top models can grind up to 720 pounds per hour. Most sporting goods retailers offer models that feature two-year warranties and have heavy-duty construction, featuring stainless steel and easily cleaned housing; grinder head and auger; a permanently lubricated motor; built-in circuit breaker with roller bearings; all metal gears; heavy duty handle; and 110-volt power. Standard accessories for all models include a large capacity meat pan, meat stamper, stainless steel grinding knife, stainless steel stuffing plate, one stainless steel fine ($\frac{3}{16}$-inch) plate, one stainless-steel coarse ($\frac{3}{8}$-inch) plate, and three stuffing tubes. The model I've been using lately is the No. 12, featuring a .75-horsepower motor and capable of grinding 360 pounds per hour.

EXTRUDERS

Ground jerky is quite commonly extruded into both snack-stick or flat-stick form, and either a hand or powered extruder is used

Ground jerky is quite often extruded into thin strips or sticks. The Hi Mountain hand-held Jerky Gun comes in a kit, the Jerky Master, that also includes a screen for drying the jerky and two flavors of Hi Mountain Cure and Seasonings. The Jerky Gun comes with two interchangeable nozzles.

for this chore. A hand extruder, such as the Jerky Gun from Hi Mountain, makes the chore quick and easy. The extruding Jerky Gun comes in a kit, the Jerky Master, which includes the gun, an industrial-grade jerky screen for drying the extruded jerky, and two flavors of Hi Mountain Jerky Cure and Seasonings. The gun is simple to use and has a swing-out tube for easy filling and cleaning. The gun comes with two interchangeable nozzles: one for strips and one for sticks. It does take some time and effort to make a fairly big batch of jerky with the hand extruder. LEM has a Jerky Cannon, and Eastman has a Jerky and Sausage Maker Gun with five tips.

(Photo courtesy Bass Pro Shops)

The LEM Jerky Cannon is a heavy-duty jerky maker, holding up to 1-½ pounds of meat at a time. The barrel is of anodized aluminum, and the ends are flared for easy loading. It comes with two stainless steel nozzles, two bags of Backwoods Seasonings, and a nylon cleaning brush.

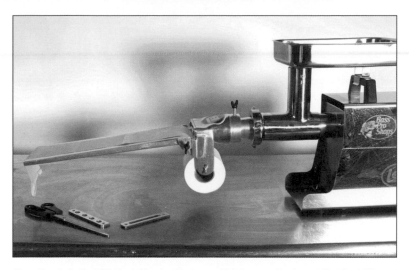

The ultimate is the LEM Meat-Shaping System, which has an attachment that fits LEM meat grinders and makes extruding jerky fast and easy. The unit comes with three stainless steel shaping plates: a wide plate for extruding square hamburger patties, a strip plate for jerky strips, and a plate with round holes for snack sticks.

(Photos courtesy Bass Pro)

If you have a large amount of ground jerky meat to mix, the LEM 17-pound manual mixer can be a great helpmate.

A powered extruder is what you want if you're making large batches of jerky. The LEM Meat-Shaping System attaches to the LEM electric grinders and can be used to quickly and easily shape a large amount of ground meat into patties, jerky strips, or snack sticks. As the meat is extruded, it comes out on a roll of waxed butcher paper. The paper roll is attached to the extruder. The extruder comes with three separate stainless steel extruding plates and a 16-inch chute. If you're into doing large batches of jerky, the LEM 17-pound manual mixer can make mixing meats and seasonings much easier than by hand.

KITCHEN SCALE

To properly mix the jerky and spices, you'll need a kitchen scale so you can weigh exact amounts of meat, especially ground meat. Most common are the 22- and 44-pound models. The 22-pound model comes with a stainless steel tray and is sufficient to weigh jerky batches. We use our digital office postal scale, which measures up to 10 pounds and works for small amounts of jerky.

(Photo courtesy Bass Pro)

Most jerky cure recipes are for specific amounts of meat. A kitchen or similar scale is necessary.

SPICES AND CURES

Making your own spice or seasoning and curing mixes for jerky is easy, but a number of companies also produce premixed jerky cures and seasonings. Hi Mountain carries a wide range of products, as do LEM Backwoods and Eastman Outdoors. These mixes are easy to use and range from such flavorings as hickory and mesquite to Hi Mountain's Inferno. If you really like hot jerky, the latter one is for you. Personally, I need cold drinks as companions for this one.

Using commercially prepared cures and seasonings is a great way to get started with jerky making, and a wide variety of different seasonings is available. Shown here are some of the mixes available from Hi Mountain.

There are a wide variety of jerky seasonings, as well as Snack Stick mix.

DEHYDRATORS

Jerky can be dried in your kitchen oven, in a dehydrator, in a smoker, or even in your barbeque grill. Using a dehydrator is the fastest way to produce jerky, and it can also be used to dry or dehydrate other food, including vegetables and fruit. We have used an Excalibur dehydrator for many years. It features five plastic mesh trays and has a thermostat that goes up to 145°F. It will dry a full load of jerky in just a few hours. The Open Country seven-tray dehydrator is an economical unit that comes with one-touch operation and a fixed temperature. The unit makes up to 7 pounds of jerky in one batch. It features a 350-watt motor and Fan Flow™ Radial Aire® for even heat distribution. The GardenMaster four-tray dehydrator puts out 1,000 watts of drying power and expands to 30 trays for 30 square feet of drying space. No tray rotation is needed. The GardenMaster

A food dehydrator does the best job of drying jerky. We've been using an Excalibur model for many years.

A number of good dehydrators are on the market these days including the Open Country economy model.

has an adjustable temperature control and comes with a packet of jerky spice and cure. LEM also has a couple of excellent dehydrators. Their six-tray unit features a rear mounted fan that distributes a directed stream of air from the 500-watt heating element. The six-tray unit has a color-coded thermostat and large trays. If you're into large batches of jerky, the LEM 10-tray stainless-steel dehydrator may be your best choice. The unit will dry up to 10 pounds of jerky at one time. The fan and 800-watt heating element are mounted in the rear of the unit, providing fast and even drying without tray rotation. An adjustable thermostat and twelve-hour timer are added features. The timer shuts off automatically when a set time has elapsed.

(Photo courtesy Bass Pro Shops)

The 10-tray stainless-steel LEM model makes drying large volumes of jerky easy.

One of the most versatile units I've tested is the Bradley Smoker. Although mine is an older unit, the new digital model offers a number of advantages. Regardless, with either unit you can hot smoke at up to 320°F, cold smoke, slow roast, or dehydrate down to 140°F. All you have to do is turn the thermostat to the desired temperature. One of the unique features of the unit is that it burns Bradley Flavor Bisquettes, preformed wood chip discs that self-load into the smoker. Precise burn time is twenty minutes per bisquette. The insulated smoking cabinet is easy to use any time of the year. Six removable racks accommodate large loads and allow heat and smoke to circulate evenly. The Bradley has an easy, front-loading design.

A Jerky Hanger holds stainless-steel skewers, enabling you to hang muscle-meat strips on the rack and dry in your oven.

(Photo courtesy Bradley Smoker)

You can also smoke-dry jerky in some smokers. I've used a Bradley Smoker for jerky making for almost ten years. The electric smoker can heat up to 320°F for serious cooking, or the thermostat can be turned down to 200°F or lower for drying the meat.

If drying in the oven, a rack, such as the LEM Jerky Hanger, has stainless steel skewers to hold strips evenly and is a much better method for drying than placing the strips on stove racks.

VACUUM PACKER

Jerky needs to stay refrigerated or even frozen for longer-term storage. Vacuum packing with a vacuum packer extends life. The better models have storage for the vacuum bag rolls and a cutter built into the unit. A wide range of units are available in a variety of prices from sporting good outlets and stores.

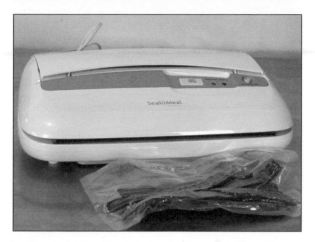

You can extend the storage time of jerky by freezing. Vacuum packing with a vacuum packer extends the frozen storage time and prevents ice crystals from forming.

MISCELLANEOUS

Items in this category include latex gloves, measuring cups and spoons, glass bowls or other non-metallic containers, resealable plastic bags or containers, cookie sheets or jerky racks for drying in

For field dressing, you'll need good latex gloves, and they can also be helpful in some butchering processes.

an oven, and a thermometer. For the thermometer, a digital model with a temperature probe that stays in meat or sausage when the oven door is shut is the best choice; an alarm sounds when the desired internal temperature is reached.

(Photo courtesy Bass Pro Shops)

A digital thermometer with a remote sensor allows you to determine the internal temperature of jerky while drying in an oven.

CHAPTER 3

Food Safety

Any type of food processing requires an understanding of safety issues and careful adherence to safe food-handling methods. This includes utilizing safe foods such as disease-free meat, safe handling steps, and safe processing. Making your own jerky or

Meat processing requires attention to safety precautions. The first is to use only meat from healthy animals, whether wild game or domestic.

drying meat is relatively simple and is, in fact, the oldest and most common form of food preservation. The technology of canning, at less than 200 years old, is relatively new. Although freezing was and is a viable preservation in areas with constant below-zero temperatures, freezing as a common food storage method only came about with the widespread availability of electricity even to rural areas.

MEAT SAFETY

The first prerequisite is safe meat. Meat should only be used from healthy, disease-free animals. It's important to be aware of diseases such as CWD (chronic wasting disease), which can be found in wild deer, elk, and moose, and BSE (bovine spongiform encephalopathy), which can be found in beef cattle, as well as the parasitic diseases of toxoplasmosis and trichinosis. According to the Wildlife Management Institute, "There is currently no evidence that CWD is transmissible to humans. However, public health officials recommend that human exposure to the CWD agent be avoided as they continue to research the disease. Although the agent that causes CWD has not been positively identified, strong evidence suggests that prions are responsible. Prions are abnormally shaped proteins that are not destroyed by cooking. Accordingly, hunters are advised not to eat meat from animals known to be infected with CWD. Research completed to date indicates that prions generally accumulate in certain parts of infected animals—the brain, eyes, spinal cord, lymph nodes, tonsils, and spleen. Based on these findings, hunters in CWD areas are advised to completely bone out harvested cervids in the field and not consume those parts of the animal where prions are likely to accumulate. Health officials advise hunters not to shoot, handle, or consume any animal that is acting abnormally or appears to be sick." In addition, they suggest hunters take normal, simple precautions such as wearing Latex gloves when field dressing a carcass. A complete list of current hunter recommendations is available at www.CWD-info.org.

Parasitic diseases can also be a problem. Toxoplasmosis is a parasitic infection caused by a protozoan known as Toxoplasma gondii. Humans most often become infected by this organism by consuming undercooked meat, especially lamb, pork, and venison, or eating unwashed fruits and vegetables. Cats, both domestic and wild, are often the carriers. A healthy person who becomes infected often experiences few symptoms, but people who have weakened immune systems are at risk of severe complications.

Trichinosis or trichinellosis is a disease caused by a parasite called Trichinella. According to the Center for Disease Control and Prevention, National Center for Infectious Diseases, Division of Parasitic Diseases, "Trichinella species have been found in

Some wild game, such as boar or bear, can carry diseases such as trichinosis. Make sure all game meat is cooked properly to 160°F internally before use.

virtually all warm-blooded animals. It's important to avoid eating undercooked meat of pork, bear, cougar, wild boar, and walrus. Make sure the meat is cooked to an internal temperature of 160°F before consumption. In the past it was thought deep freezing for 30 days or more killed the parasite, but trichinella in bear meat is not killed by freezing. Commercially, irradiation is used to kill the parasite. Smoking, drying, curing, or microwaving does not consistently kill the infective trichinella worms."

Meat that is tainted, unsafely butchered, and cut up also poses serious health problems, especially from E. coli. When I was a kid back in the 1940s, I used to watch the community butchering processes as neighbors came in and everyone worked together to butcher hogs. My dad told the story about a mishap when a piece

Unsafe field dressing of wild game can be a problem, causing dangerous diseases such as E. coli. Make sure you field dress using all efforts to prevent contamination of the meat with intestinal fluids.

of meat fell off the cutting table onto the ground where the hog scalding and scraping had occurred and was covered with hair. "One that eats the most sausage gets the most hair," a neighbor joked as the scrap was quickly eaten by the neighbor's dog. Food poisoning by E. coli, however, is no joke. It's a serious health problem that can make you extremely ill and can even kill you. E. coli is a bacterium that commonly lives in the intestines of people and animals. Many strains of E. coli exist: Most are normal inhabitants of the small intestines and colon, and are non-pathogenic. This means they do not cause disease in the intestines. E. coli 0157:H7, however, is a dangerous, disease-causing bacterium coming mostly from poorly cooked meat—most commonly, hamburger; for that reason, the disease is often called "hamburger disease." E. coli causes bloody diarrhea, cramps, and a blood and kidney disease in children. The most common cause of the disease is contamination of the meat from intestinal fluids that are spilled or smeared on the meat during field dressing or butchering. This is especially so when the meat is then ground and the contamination is spread throughout the meat. Make sure all meat is cooked to 160°F before drying.

FIELD DRESSING

If you're making jerky from wild game such as deer or elk, the chances are you'll be field dressing and butchering the game as well. And there is no reason you shouldn't do all your own processing: It's not complicated and safety is not an issue if you follow common-sense rules. Use the proper steps in field dressing and caring for the carcass, and then make sure the meat is processed properly. If you process all your own meat, you will know exactly what you and your family are eating. Field dress wild game as soon as possible to allow the body heat to dissipate rapidly. Venison can be contaminated with fecal bacteria—the degree varying with the hunter's skill, location of the wound, and other factors. Take all necessary steps to avoid puncturing the digestive tract—a common problem caused by not cutting around and tying off the anus during field dressing, or cutting into the intestines when opening the abdominal cavity. A sharp, gut-hook knife helps avoid the problem. If the animal has been gut-shot, however, then you will have a problem. Remove as much digestive material as possible, and thoroughly wash out the cavity with lots of running water. Then, cut away and discard any meat that has been tainted during the butchering process. Thoroughly clean and disinfect the knife before further use. Do not cut through any organs you suspect may contain disease.

A hunting knife with a gut hook can be helpful in preventing contamination during field dressing.

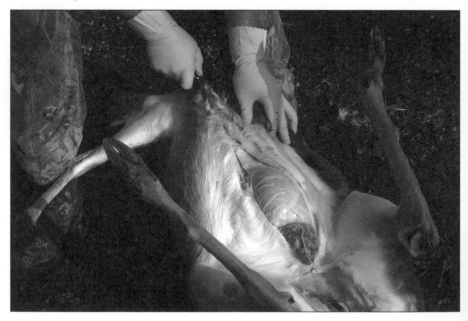

AGING

If the weather is suitable—not above 45°F—you may wish to skin and hang the carcass for a few days to age the meat. (Aging will not only improve the meat's flavor, but it will make it more tender.) If this is not feasible, cut the carcass into quarters and age it in a refrigerator set between 35°F and 40°F for about a week. (These low temperatures are necessary to reduce potential contamination of the meat.) Blood will pool on the lower ends, so make sure you place the pieces upright in pans and drain away the excess blood daily. It is not unusual for our family and friends to have a half dozen deer down on opening day, and here in the Ozarks, the daytime temperatures during November can be in the 70s. Several years ago, I found an old refrigerator truck body for sale at a restau-

The carcass must be skinned and chilled as quickly as possible, and it must be kept below 45°F to age or until you cut it up.

rant that was going out of business. For a couple of hundred bucks and a little help from a buddy and his flatbed trailer, we acquired the ultimate: a giant refrigerator. Now, when the weather is warm, we use the unit to hang everyone's deer to age, as well as to hold quantities of meat in covered tubs as we process everything.

CLEANING AND DISINFECTING

One of the most important facets of all steps in butchering and meat processing is to keep everything clean and disinfected. This includes work surfaces such as tables, countertops, and cutting boards. Make sure to thoroughly clean and disinfect knives, grinders, extruders, and any other tools that come into contact with the meat. Clean all surfaces with extremely hot, soapy water with a little bleach added. Remove soap with hot clean water. A solution of bleach, soap, and water kept in a spray bottle can also be useful for quickly cleaning

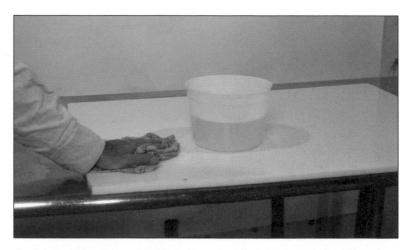

Keeping everything clean and disinfected is an important step in meat processing. Always wash all working surfaces and tools before and after use with hot soapy water, and then rinse it with hot clean water.

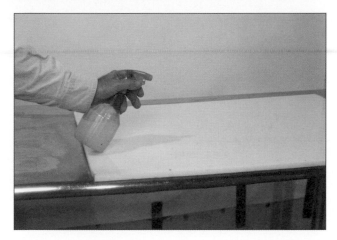

A solution of bleach, water, and soap in a spray bottle can be used to disinfect surfaces and tools.

Cutting boards used with raw meat should not be used for cutting other foods.

surfaces and equipment. Always follow by rinsing with hot clean water. Be sure to clean and sanitize all equipment before using, after using, and before storing away.

BUTCHERING

My favorite butchering method for making deer into jerky is to bone off all meat while the carcass is still hanging. This prevents the possibility of contamination from pathogens found in the brain and spinal column when cutting through them with a meat saw, and results in a pile of boneless meat, the loins going into the freezer for steaks, and the rest to be ground for ground jerky, sausage, and burger meat. A rump or two is left as whole muscle meat to be sliced into jerky as well.

The carcass should be hanging head down, and the first step is to skin the carcass (if not already done). I like to use a rope winch

Boning the meat from the carcass not only avoids cutting through bones and potential pathogen problems, but it is easier than using a meat saw. The front shoulder is easily removed by slicing from the carcass.

in order to lower or raise the carcass as I work on the different parts. The skin can be removed with or without cutting off the head and front feet. One method is to skin down to the head and cut it off at the neck. Then, skin down to the front feet and cut them off with a meat saw. You can also skin down to the head and cut off the skin at the joint between the head and neck. Cut from inside the skin to help prevent getting hair on the carcass. Skin down to the hocks and encircle the legs with a cut to remove the skin from the legs. The latter avoids using a meat saw completely, but it requires a bit more skinning effort.

Using a sharp boning knife, separate a shoulder from the carcass. There is no connecting bone joint between the shoulder and the body. Simply pull the front leg out and away from the carcass and slice it off. Lay this shoulder aside and remove the other. Again, using a good boning knife, simply cut all the meat away from the shoulder bone and leg. The bottom portion of the

Then simply cut around the bone with a sharp knife to debone.

The shoulder bone has a sharp ridge on one side. Cut in around it to remove the meat.

The result is a pile of boneless meat.

leg is filled with sinew and is quite tough. I usually add this to another pile to be used as dog food (cooked first) for our labs, but it can be ground with a sharp grinder. Note that there is a sharp ridge of bone on the outside of the shoulder that must be cut around to obtain all the meat from the side. Place these boned-out

Continue deboning the carcass. Cutting off the flank steak is shown here.

pieces in a clean, covered tub and refrigerate until you can slice or grind them.

Remove the backstrap or loin by cutting down either side of the backbone, then cutting from the rib side to release the long strip of meat. Properly cut, the loin will peel out fairly simply. Cut away the other backstrap in the same manner. This choice piece

Remove the loins by cutting down along the backbone, then making a cut from the rib side and peeling it out.

of meat can be cut into muscle-meat strips or ground for jerky, but we like to save it for the grill. Don't forget to cut and peel the small tenderloin pieces located inside the carcass next to the backbone. Cut away the brisket meat, as well as the layer of meat joining the ribs and the backbone. Then, simply cut away all neck meat, leaving the neck bone. This is tougher meat that requires keeping the knife sharp. My nephew is a jerky nut and he actually bones out the meat between each rib. I find this meat has a lot of fat, which must be trimmed away for grinding, so I usually leave it in place to be discarded with the carcass.

The hams or hindquarters provide the most meat for jerky and are also boned out while the carcass is still hanging. Don't worry about keeping specific pieces separate, as you would with labeled, traditional butchering. If there was any spillage of intestinal fluids

The backstrap or loin offers a choice piece of meat that can be used for steaks or sliced into muscle-meat jerky.

The loin has a layer of fat on the outside that should be peeled off.

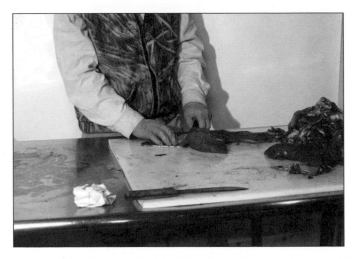

A layer of tough sinew also covers the loin. (This was a major source of sinew that Native Americans used for many items.) Using a boning knife, start a cut between the meat and sinew, then turn the loin sinew-side down on a smooth, flat surface and slice it with a sharp knife, much like filleting a fish.

around the aitchbone or anus area, it will be on the exposed ends of the hindquarters next to the bone. Trim these pieces away, and then wash the knife and sterilize it. Make a cut starting at the top of the hindquarter and simply follow the bone down to the aitchbone area. Make a cut down the aitchbone to meet the first cut. Then continue cutting around the bone until you have all meat removed. You're now left with a completely boned-out carcass and a good amount of boneless meat ready to grind or slice into jerky—and there are no bones to take up excess space in your refrigerator or freezer.

Again, these boned-out pieces must be kept well refrigerated until they can be sliced into jerky pieces or ground for jerky. Do not wait overly long as even refrigerated meat won't last forever. Cut up or grind within three days.

SLICING AND CHUNKING

The next step is to cut up the meat, either into strips for jerky or into chunks to be ground. Regardless of whether the meat is to be cut into strips or chunks, it's important to cut away all fat and as much gristle and sinew as possible. The former doesn't create a safety problem, but fat in deer adds an off taste. Gristle and sinew make the meat tough. Also, make sure you cut away all bloody meat parts and discard. Always thoroughly wash your hands before and after you handle raw meat. Do not use cutting boards for meat and other foods, but keep meat-only boards. Clean and sanitize often.

Other safety steps must also be followed. Keep meat and poultry refrigerated below 40°F. Use or freeze ground beef and poultry within two days and whole red meats within three to five days. Defrost frozen meat in the refrigerator, not on the counter, to prevent any contamination or spoilage. Marinate meat in the refrigerator, and discard leftover marinades.

DRYING

The next safety issue is properly drying the meat. According to the USDA, "The scientific principal of preserving food by drying is that by removing moisture, enzymes cannot efficiently contact or react with the food. Whether these enzymes are bacterial, fungal or naturally occurring autolytic enzymes from the raw food, preventing this enzymatic action preserves the food from biological action."

Several different methods of drying can be or have been used, including natural drying, solar drying, and drying by the use of an artificially generated heat source. Natural drying includes sun drying and "adiabatic" or shade drying. Both of these ancient and traditional methods are done in the open air. Natural drying requires a windy climate with a dry heat, and even then, chances for improper drying are great. This is a survival-only method and should not be attempted by the home jerky maker. Solar drying utilizes a drier that catches the sun and creates heat for the drying process. These passive driers often do not reach temperatures high enough to kill some pathogens. Solar driers are more commonly used for fruits and vegetables, including apples, apricots, peaches, grapes, bananas, tomatoes, peppers, zucchini, and others.

The third type, drying by an artificially generated heat, is done by placing the meat in a warm oven, electric food dehydrator, or even some smokers or other heat sources. An oven will dry jerky, but it will not dehydrate the meat as quickly as a dehydrator because of the lack of air circulation. Do not attempt to dry meats in a microwave. You'll only cook the meat, not dry it out, and again, there is no air convection or circulation.

A food dehydrator consists of a source of heat, a fan to circulate the dry air, and trays or other means, including mesh sheets, to hold the meat during the process. A food dehydrator used for making jerky must have an adjustable temperature dial and be able to maintain a temperature of at least 140°F throughout the drying process. It's a good idea to regularly shift the trays from top to bottom to ensure even drying, that there is only one layer of meat per tray, and that no pieces are touching or overlapping.

Smokers that can achieve the desired temperatures, and maintain them properly without overheating and cooking the meat, can also be used. Smoking can also add more flavor to the jerky. Electric smokers with adjustable temperature controls up to 200°F or over are a good choice. Use only proper smoking woods or chips, such as apple, hickory, alder, or mesquite. Soft woods such as pine contain resins and compounds that not only provide an off flavor but are dangerous.

The possibility of illnesses due to salmonella and E. coli 0157:H7 from homemade jerky raises questions about the safety of traditional drying methods for making beef and venison jerky.

Another safety issue is proper drying of the jerky. Red meat such as beef and venison must be heated to 160°F internally. Poultry must be heated to a minimum of 165°F. Steam, boil, or roast meats while measuring the internal temperature with a meat thermometer.

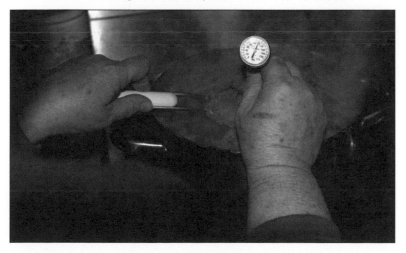

The amount of time jerky can be stored depends on the method used to cure and dry, the relative humidity, air temperature, and other factors. Store in a cool, dry place in a tightly closed container.

The USDA Meat and Poultry Hotline's current recommendation for making jerky safely is to heat red meat such as beef and venison to 160°F internally; turkey, duck, and other poultry must be heated to a minimum of 165°F internally; and fish should be heated to 140°F to kill parasites. This step ensures that any bacteria present will be destroyed by wet heat. Most dehydrator and/or jerky-cure products do not include this step, and a dehydrator may not reach temperatures high enough to heat the various meats to the proper temperatures. To counter this, steam or roast meats to 160°F internally and poultry to 165°F internally before dehydrating it. Use a digital meat thermometer to assure the proper temperatures.

The danger in dehydrating meat and poultry without first cooking it to a safe temperature is that the appliance may not heat the meat to 160°F and poultry to 165°F—the temperatures at which bacteria are destroyed—before it dries. Bacteria become much more heat resistant after drying. The problem is that evaporating

Larger quantities of jerky can be frozen for longer storage times.

moisture absorbs most of the heat in a low-temperature oven or dehydrator. The internal temperature of the meat does not begin to rise until most of the moisture has evaporated. When the dried meat temperature finally begins to rise, the bacteria have become more heat resistant and are more likely to survive. If the surviving bacteria are pathogenic, they can cause foodborne illness to those eating the jerky.

After heating, maintain a constant dehydrator temperature of 130°F to 140°F in order to dry the food fast enough before it spoils and remove enough water that microorganisms are unable to grow.

According to the National Center for Home Food Preservation, "If the strips were not heated in marinade prior to drying, they can be heated in an oven after drying as an added safety measure. Place strips on a baking sheet, close together, but not touching or overlapping. For strips originally cut one-quarter-inch thick or less, heat them for 10 minutes in an oven preheated to 275°F. (Thicker strips may require longer heating to reach 160°F.)"

Vacuum packing can also add to storage time.

Depending on the methods used, including cures and mixes, homemade jerky can normally be kept stored for up to two months, although some types may last only a few days and some not at all without refrigeration. The storage time also depends on the time of year, the relative moisture in the air, and the cure used. Jerky can also be frozen and kept for longer periods. Jerky will, however, take up moisture from the frost when removed from the freezer and must be consumed promptly. For that reason, only remove an amount you will consume in a few days from the freezer at a time. You can add storage time to both frozen and unfrozen jerky by vacuum packing it with a vacuum packer. One problem with this method is the sharp edges and corners of the dried meat may poke holes in the plastic bags.

CHAPTER 4

Old-Time Jerky Making

No matter what the main ingredient was or is—mastodon, elk, deer, African or Australian game, beef, fish, you name it—the old-fashioned method of making jerky has been around for a long time. Old-time jerky is still easy to make and still provides a great food source. In the old days, jerky making was very simple. The Native Americans simply cut thin strips of meat from game they had killed, then hung the strips over racks made of thin branches. In the dry Southwest and the Plains, meat dried quickly and easily with the use of this method. In the North, a small, smoky fire was often used to speed the drying process. Not only did this help the drying process, but it also kept away the blowflies. In the North-west, smoke houses were constructed to protect the meat and aid in the drying process. If the Native Americans had access to salt, it was applied as well. The Native Americans also dried salmon, placing them on long racks as they removed fish from the fish wheels in the rivers.

One of my favorite outdoor writers from earlier days was Colonel Townsend Whelen. This is his description of jerky making:

The old-time method of jerky making using only the sun has been a tradition in many cultures, including those of the American West.

Jerky is lean meat cut in strips and dried over a fire or in the sun. Cut the lean, fresh red meat in long, wide strips about half an inch thick. Hang these on a framework about 4 to 6 feet off the ground. Under the rack, build a small, slow, smoky fire of any non-resinous wood. Let the meat dry in the sun and wind. Cover it at night or in rain. It should dry in several days.

The fire should not be hot enough to cook the meat since its chief use is to keep flies away. When jerked, the meat will be hard, more or less black outside, and will keep almost indefinitely away from damp and flies.

It is best eaten just as it is; just bite off a chunk and chew. Eaten thus, it is quite tasty. It may also be cooked in stews and is very concentrated and nourishing. A little goes a long way as an emergency ration, but alone it is not good food for long, continued consumption, as it lacks the necessary fat.

Following is a campsite jerky technique I learned from an old-time Wyoming big-game guide. He described his method of making jerky to me as we chewed on some while glassing for elk:

Cut the meat into strips, lay on a flat surface, and sprinkle both sides with black pepper. Lightly sprinkle with salt. Rub the salt and pepper well into all sides of the strips. Cut holes in the ends of the strips and thread white cotton or butchers cord through each hole, tying off into loops. Bring a pot of water to boil and immerse the strips into the boiling water for 15 to 20 seconds, remove, then re-dip.

The traditional Native American method of drying meat for jerky consisted of hanging meat strips over racks made of thin branches. A small, smoky fire under the meat not only kept away insects but also added flavor and aided in the drying process.

One old-time method of preheating jerky strips was to place loops of string through holes cut in the ends of the strips. These were threaded onto a stick and dipped in a pot of boiling water.

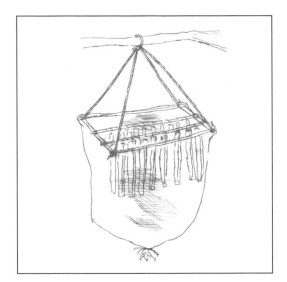

A bag or "tent" of cheesecloth was often used to help keep off insects while the jerky dried.

Hang the strips to dry. If the strips are hung outside in the sunshine, cover them with a cheesecloth tent to keep off insects and make sure they're high enough so dogs and other critters can't get to them. The strips can also be hung on clothesline in a cold, dry room. The strips should be dry in 4 to 5 days.

Another traditional method involves the use of curing salt, an old-time product. It's easy to make your own curing salt. Take 1 pound of canning salt, 6 ounces of Prague powder, 3 ounces of sugar, and 2 ounces of white pepper. You can substitute brown sugar and black pepper. If you like hot jerky, add ground red pepper or cayenne pepper to suit. Mix all together and rub the mix over all the meat slices. Leave in a cool place overnight, then dry. In damp weather, the slices can be dried in an oven or meat smoker.

An old-time oven method is to lay strips in a glass dish, place a drop of Liquid Smoke over each strip, and use a pastry brush to evenly coat each strip. Sprinkle seasoning salt and seasoned pepper over the layer. Add a light sprinkling of sugar and garlic powder if you like garlic. Add another layer of strips, brush with Liquid Smoke, sprinkle with salt and pepper, then add another layer of strips. Continue adding and seasoning until the dish is full or you run out of strips. Cover the dish and set in a refrigerator or cool area (below 40°F) overnight. Dry in an oven set to 200°F or in a dehydrator.

PEMMICAN

Made from jerky, pemmican was also a staple food of the Native Americans. Another of my favorite old-time writers, George Leonard Herter, in his *Professional Guides' Manual*, published in 1966, stated, "Pemmican properly made is one of the finest foods that you can take into the wilderness or for a survival food in case of atomic bombing. Pemmican keeps indefinitely. Today, in our wonderful atomic age, pemmican is part of the survival ration of the newest United States Air Corps jet bombers."

According to Col. Townsend Whelen, "To make pemmican you start with jerky and shred it by pounding. Then, take a lot of raw animal fat, cut it into small pieces about the size of walnuts, and fry these out in a pan over a slow fire, not letting the grease boil up. When the grease is all out of the lumps, discard these and pour the hot fat over the shredded jerky, mixing the two together until you have about the consistency of ordinary sausage. Then, pack the pemmican in waterproof bags. The Indians used skin bags."

The proportions should be about half lean meat and half rendered fat. The Native Americans also added fruits such as wild grapes, dried berries and beans, corn, herbs, and other items. These added vitamin C, which prevents scurvy as well as other nutrients and gave the pemmican different tastes. To use, place the dried block of pemmican in water and bring to a boil. Herter suggests dropping in some chili powder, soaking some beans over-night, adding them, and then "You will have an excellent chili con carne."

If you want to try making pemmican, the following is a recipe to make approximately 10 pounds.

5 lb. jerky
½ lb. brown sugar
¾ lb. raisins or dried currents
4 lb. melted fat

Pound the jerky until it crumbles, and mix all ingredients together.

If you want to make a more modern version, first run the jerky through a food processor. Then, add ½ cup of raisins, ½ cup of salted peanuts, and ½ cup brown sugar for each pound of jerky.

Jerky was often made into pemmican by the Native Americans, utilizing suet cooked to render off the fat, then adding the fat, as well as fruits, herbs, and other ingredients to jerky that had been pulverized. Today you can use a food processor to quickly pulverize the jerky.

Other dried fruits such as cranberries can also be used. Sugar is optional, a matter of taste. The sugar can also be replaced with chocolate or any other flavor of chips (butterscotch, semi-sweet, milk chocolate, and so on). Press the mixture into a pan, packing tightly. Pour melted suet or other fat over the mixture, using only enough fat to hold the ingredients together. It's easy to get too much fat. A modern alternative to melted suet or bacon grease is a butter-flavored shortening. Allow the mixture to cool and then cut into squares for storage and use.

To make a chili version, leave out the sugar and dried fruit and stir in chili seasoning with the ground jerky and fat. To use, add a chunk of the chili-flavored pemmican to a pot of cooking beans. This makes a very hardy camp meal.

For long-term storage, it's best to keep your jerky supply in the freezer and make pemmican just before consuming. Except

Add raisins or other dried fruits and nuts to the pulverized jerky, then stir in the warm, melted fat, adding only enough fat to hold the mixture together. A butter-flavored shortening is a good alternative to bacon grease or rendered suet.

for short periods of time, keep pemmican in the refrigerator, especially in warm weather.

It's possible to make jerky and pemmican using these age-old traditional methods, even in a remote camp, but always follow the safe food processing issues discussed in Chapter 3.

CHAPTER

Sliced Muscle-Meat Jerky

The simplest, traditional, method of producing jerky is to use sliced muscle meat. Almost any type of big-game meat can be sliced into jerky, including wild game such as deer, elk, moose, sheep, and antelope. Other meats, such as wild turkey breast,

Traditional jerky was, and still is, made by cutting muscle meat into slices. Wild game such as deer and elk were and are popular meat choices. Beef is a traditional meat, while the Native Americans utilized buffalo.

can also be made into jerky slices. Beef is a traditional sliced-jerky meat in many parts of the world, and buffalo was a favorite of early settlers and Native Americans.

In the 1970s I was a young freelance writer and book author with a family to feed. Since we lived on a farm in the Ozarks, venison was a regular food staple. I started making jerky in the old-fashioned, sliced muscle-meat method back then and have been doing so ever since. With several deer usually taken each season, most of one deer would end up being turned into jerky.

TRIMMING AND SLICING

Traditionally I've used the hams or rear quarters of venison for old-fashioned, sliced jerky. The hams do provide good meat cuts for other uses, including roasts and hamburgers, but they also slice

Once the meat has been deboned from the carcass, cut it into long chunks, following the sinew or natural muscle divisions.

Cut away all fat and sinew.

extremely well for jerky. Then, I use the butcher trimmings, left from cutting the sliced jerky, for ground meat, both for jerky and to cook in chili, tacos, meatloaf, and so forth. Once the rear quarters have been deboned from the carcass, cut the meat into long chunks by simply following the muscles where they are separated by sinew. Cut away any fat, as fat not only doesn't dry properly, but it adds a gamey flavor to the meat. Also cut away as much sinew as possible. Next, using a sharp butcher knife, slice the meat into thin strips, following the grain, not across it. Slice into strips either ⅛- or ¼-inch thick. Strips can actually be cut as thick as ⅜ inch, but any thicker and they become extremely hard to dry. The thickness is actually only a matter of taste. It takes longer to dry and cure the thicker strips, but they also tend to turn out less brittle when dried.

Then, slice into strips of the desired thickness.

The Hi Mountain Jerky Board and stainless steel knife makes it easier to more consistenly slice meat to the correct thickness and therefore results in a more consistent drying of the jerky. If a strip of meat is ⅛ inch at one end and ⅜ inch at the opposite end, for instance, it will be difficult for it to dry evenly. The board comes with a lip around the edge that allows you to slice ⅛- or ¼-inch thicknesses. Place the meat on the board and slice holding the knife with the flat side of the blade down on the edge lips.

The simplest and most consistent method of slicing meat is with an electric slicer. Regardless of the method used, for easier slicing, lay the trimmed meat pieces on a cookie sheet or other flat surface, place in the freezer until the meat is partially frozen, (usually about an hour to hour and a half) and then slice.

The Hi Mountain slicing kit includes a wooden board with raised edges to help guide the stainless steel knife (included) for precise ⅛- or ¼-inch slices.

Place the meat to be sliced in the board, and slide the knife (flat side down) along the raised edges.

Frequently dipping the knife blade in cold water assists in slicing.

An electric slicer can be used to cut precise thickness slices fast.

CURING

Jerky can be nothing more than dried meat using a variety of heat and drying sources. Curing the jerky meat, however, not only adds to the preservation but improves the flavor. Jerky can also be made with a wide range of flavorings, depending on the seasonings and spices used. You can make up your own curing recipes, or use some of the wide range of cures and seasoning mixes available commercially. The latter often contain nitrites to aid in curing. Make sure you follow the recipe and use the proper amount of cure so you don't have too little or too much nitrite. In order to use any recipe, homemade or commercial, you need to know the exact weight of the sliced meat. Regardless, the commercially prepared cures and mixes allow you to make your own jerky with proven taste results. On the other hand, experimenting with homemade recipes is half the fun of making jerky.

The meat can simply be dried, but in most instances, a cure or seasoning is added for flavor and can also be used to help cure the meat. You can make your own cure and seasonings by using a variety of curing agents and spices.

For most cure and seasoning mixes, you must know the exact amount of meat you're dealing with. We use our postal scale to weigh up to 10 pounds of meat.

Curing can be accomplished by using one of two methods: marinating the meat in a liquid marinade or using a dry rub to coat the meat. In most instances, the meat must sit a length of time before drying in order for the cure to work through. I've used both methods with good results.

The following recipes are primarily for venison, but elk, moose, antelope, or beef could be substituted.

MARINADES

Lawry Marinade

2 lb. meat, thinly sliced
⅔ cup Lawry's Seasoned Marinade or Mesquite Marinade

This is one of the simplest recipes I've used. Place ⅔ cup of Lawry's Seasoned Marinade or Mesquite Marinade and 2 lb. of meat strips in a resealable plastic bag or sealable plastic container. Mix until all meat strips are evenly coated. Place in the refrigerator for 2 to 4 hours. Remove, allow the meat strips to drain on paper towels, and then pat the surface dry with more paper towels. Sprinkle on Lawry's Seasoned Pepper or Garlic Pepper.

To dry, turn on an oven to 200°F, prop the door open an inch or so, and dry the meat. Drying can take anywhere from 2 to 6 hours. Check often for doneness. Jerky strips should feel like leather and bend but not break. The meat should be dried but not cooked. Store in an airtight container and keep in a cool, dry place.

Burch Marinade No. 1

2 lb. meat, thinly sliced
1 cup of soy sauce
1 tablespoon garlic powder
1 tablespoon onion powder
Water to cover

The meat can be cured in one of two methods. Using a liquid marinade is very common.

The dry cure and spices are mixed with enough water or liquid to cover the meat.

Allow the meat to soak in the liquid in a non-metallic container, usually overnight.

I've used this simple marinade for almost 40 years. Many recipes contain salt as a curing agent, but other ingredients can be used to replace the salt. Soy sauce is substituted for the salt in this recipe. Mix the ingredients; place them with the meat in a glass bowl, plastic container, or resealable plastic bag; and refrigerate for 12 hours or overnight. Remove, drain, and pat dry. Dry in the oven or a dehydrator. If you desire a spicier taste, add Tabasco Sauce.

Burch Marinade No. 2

2 lb. meat, thinly sliced
Water to cover
1 tablespoon Worcestershire sauce
1 tablespoon salt
½ cup brown sugar
½ teaspoon black pepper
2 tablespoons onion powder or one large, fresh onion, finely diced
1 teaspoon garlic powder
Tabasco sauce to taste

Jerky is marinated to provide the taste and can be made as spicy or as mild as you prefer. Above is a very mild recipe we've used for years. Once the meat is sliced and all fat removed, place it in freezer bags, freeze for 60 days at 0°F to 5°F, and then cure and dry in an oven or dehydrator.

Place the thinly sliced meat in a bowl, cover with the marinade, and refrigerate for at least 24 hours. Stir occasionally. You can make the marinade spicier by adding soy sauce or teriyaki sauce and hotter by adding ground red pepper. Some folks like to add more sugar. You can also simply sprinkle additional spices onto the meat before drying, if you want even more flavor.

DRY RUB CURES

Dry rub cures normally consist of the dry ingredients sprinkled over and rubbed into the meat. The rub ingredients are then allowed time to work into the meat before drying.

Easy-Does-It Oven Jerky

Meat, thinly sliced
Liquid Smoke
Seasoned salt

This is a great recipe if you just want to try your hand at making jerky without a lot of hassle and ingredients. It's quick, easy, and tasty. All you'll need is meat, Liquid Smoke, and seasoned salt. Slice the meat into ⅛-inch-thick pieces. Brush a bit of Liquid Smoke on both sides of each piece and then dust each piece with seasoned salt. Place the coated meat strips in a covered container or sealable plastic bag and store in a refrigerator. Allow the strips to marinate overnight. Remove and pat dry with paper towels to get rid of any excess moisture. Place cookie sheets or aluminum foil on the bottom of the oven to catch any dripping. Spray the oven racks with cooking oil and then hang the meat slices over the racks. Set the oven to 200°F and roast the meat until liquid begins to drip. Reduce the heat to 140°F, and dry the meat with the oven door slightly open. The jerky should be ready in 4 to 6 hours, but test frequently.

Morton Salt Jerky

2 lb. lean beef or game, sliced
2 tablespoons Morton Tender Quick mix or Morton Sugar Cure
    mix in plain

2 teaspoons sugar
1 teaspoon ground black pepper
1 teaspoon garlic powder

One simple and easy dry-rub cure recipe I've used with extremely good results is the Morton salt jerky recipe. It is extremely mild yet long lasting.

In a small bowl, stir together the Morton Tender Quick mix or Morton Sugar Cure mix and the remaining ingredients. Place the meat on a clean surface or on a large flat pan, and rub all surfaces with the cure mixture. You can also put the ingredients in a bowl, and then rub the cure into each slice of meat. Place the rubbed strips in a plastic food storage bag, and seal shut. Allow to cure in the refrigerator for at least 1 hour. After curing, rinse strips under cold running water and pat dry with paper towels. Arrange

A dry-rub technique can also be used. Mix the ingredients thoroughly.

Sprinkle the ingredients over the meat strips and toss to coat well, or rub the mix into the meat surfaces.

Place the rubbed strips in a glass or plastic container or zippered plastic bag to cure.

meat strips on a single layer on greased racks in a shallow baking pan. Meat edges should not overlap. Place in a 325°F oven, and cook meat to an internal temperature of 160°F. Dry meat in a home dehydrator following the manufacturer's instructions.

Venison Jerky—Chef William's Style

2 lb. venison roast
Cajun Injector Wild Game Marinade: Cane Syrup Recipe
Vegetable oil
Cajun Injector Cajun Shake

One of the most unusual jerky recipes is a combination of marinade and dry rub. This recipe is from Chef Williams, the founder of Cajun Injector Marinades. We found the recipe in an old pamphlet from Cajun Injector and have used it for years. The company doesn't make the Cane Syrup Recipe Marinade anymore, but their other marinades, such as Teriyaki and Honey, also work well with this recipe.

Inject the roast using 2 ounces of Cajun Injector Wild Game Marinade per pound of meat. Slice the roast into ⅛- to ¼-inch slices, slicing with the grain. Sprinkle with Cajun Shake. Brown the venison strips in hot oil in a large skillet, turning as the strips brown. Place in a dish and cover the strips with 8 ounces of Cajun Injector Wild Game Marinade and sprinkle with the Cajun Shake. Let the strips sit overnight in a refrigerator. Drain off the marinade and pat dry. Dry in a dehydrator or bake in a 150°F oven with door partially open for 8 hours or until the meat is dry.

USING PREPARED CURES AND MIXES

I've experimented with a number of prepared cures and mixes and found them easy and fun to use. In all cases, the product comes in two packages: a cure and a seasoning. It's extremely important to follow the mixture amounts suggested by the manufacturer for the specific poundage of meat. It's also a good idea to make up small batches of jerky to test for taste. The following are jerky-making suggestions and methods from the products I've tested.

Uncle Buck's Jerky Regular Seasoning and Cure

Up to 10 lb. meat
2 cups water for every 2 lb. meat
8 teaspoons seasoning for every 2 lb. meat
½ teaspoon cure for every 2 lb. meat

Cut the meat strips ⅛-inch-thick and 8 inches long. To cure up to 10 pounds of meat, mix the cure packet and seasoning with 5 cups of water. For smaller batches, mix 8 teaspoons seasoning, ½ teaspoon of cure, 2 cups of water, and 2 pounds of meat strips. Mix

Uncle Buck's Jerky Seasoning and Cure provides a great way of making jerky with a sure-fire recipe.

Place the cure mix in water.

Add the seasoning mix and stir well.

Add the strips.

Stir well and refrigerate for 8 hours.

well and marinate strips in solution for 8 hours under refrigeration. Hang strips in oven at lowest setting with door open to the first stop until jerky reaches desired dryness. A dehydrator may also be used. This product is also available in hickory and mesquite flavors.

Eastman Outdoors Jerky Cure and Seasoning

Lean meat
3 teaspoons seasoning for every 1 lb. of meat
1 teaspoon for every 1 lb. of meat
Cure

Start with the leanest meat possible. Trim excess fat and partially freeze the meat for easier slicing. Cut along the grain into strips no more than ⅜-inch thick. Weigh the strips to determine how much seasoning and cure to use. Then follow the mixing chart using standard measuring spoons and a non-metallic bowl, mixing 3 teaspoons of seasoning and 1 level teaspoon of cure for each pound of meat. Gently toss the strips with the mixture. For best results, use the Eastman Outdoors Reveo to infuse maximum flavor into the meat. Cover the bowl, or place strips in a sealable plastic bag, and refrigerate for at least 24 hours. Use an oven, smoker, or dehydrator to dry. The Eastman Outdoors products are available in original, hickory, teriyaki, mesquite, and whiskey pepper.

Hi Mountain Jerky Cure and Seasonings

Hi Mountain Jerky Cure and Seasonings are old recipes, made without preservatives, and the dried jerky must be kept frozen or refrigerated. The company suggests you have fun with jerky. If you have meat that has been in the freezer for a while, for example, don't waste it: make it into jerky instead. Or, if you have a roast, try cutting it into 1-inch squares, and make jerky nuggets. Hi Mountain products are available in ten authentic Western recipes: original blend, pepper, mesquite, hickory, mandarin teriyaki, bourbon BBQ, cajun, cracked pepper and garlic, inferno, and pepperoni.

Cut the meat into strips of desired lengths and widths, allowing for shrinkage. Weigh the meat after cutting into strips and trimming. Now you know the exact amount of mix to use. Mix the spices, and cure according to the spice and cure mixing chart. Mix only the amount you need. Be sure to store the remaining unmixed spices and cure in an airtight container until needed. Hi Mountain recommends that you always make sure you mix the cure and seasonings exactly and correctly. Fluff the cure and seasoning before measuring. Always use standard measuring spoons, level full. Scrape off excess cure or seasoning with a table knife, leaving the measuring spoon level. Do not compact.

Hi Mountain provides a wide variety of flavors in their line of cure and seasoning mixes that can be used with sliced jerky.

The cure and seasoning spices must be mixed together precisely according to the amount of meat being treated.

Hi Mountain provides a shaker bottle to apply their mixes. Apply to one side of the meat, turn, and apply to the opposite.

Thoroughly mix the meat and spices in a non-metallic bowl.

Place the slices in a non-metallic container or zippered plastic bag and refrigerate for the time specified by the recipe.

Lay the strips flat on an even surface. (If you have just washed the game meat, be sure to pat it dry before applying the cure and seasoning.) Using the blended spices and cure, apply to the prepared meat using the shaker bottle enclosed with the mixes. Sprinkle the first side of the meat strips with approximately half of the measured mix. Turn the meat strips over and sprinkle the remaining mix on the meat strips. If you can't get an even distribution on the meat, especially on the ends and edges, put all the seasoned strips in a large mixing bowl and tumble by hand until the cure and seasoning have been spread evenly over the entire batch.

Stack the strips, pressed together tightly, in a non-metallic container or a resealable plastic bag and refrigerate for at least 24 hours. Hi Mountain Jerky Cure and Seasoning is specially formulated to penetrate meat at the rate of $\frac{1}{4}$ inch per 24 hours. If thicker pieces of meat are used, increase curing time accordingly; for instance, cure $\frac{3}{8}$-inch-thick strips for approximately 28 hours. Do not cure any meat less than 24 hours.

DRYING

The following instruction for cooking or smoking jerky is from Hi Mountain: "Place foil or pan on bottom of oven to catch drippings. Lay the strips on the oven racks, making sure there is air between each piece (our Jerky Screens are perfect here). Place in the oven for 1 to 1¼ hours at 200°F with the oven door open just a crack. Taste the jerky frequently. When the jerky is cooked to your liking, stop cooking. The jerky is made with cure and seasonings, it does not have to be dry to the point where you can't chew it like store bought jerky. Remember, taste often while cooking or smoking."

Our oven door won't stay open just a crack, so I keep the door open with a wooden clothespin. A wooden stick of the desired thickness would also work. Another easy oven-dry technique is to

The jerky strips can be dried in several ways. The first step, however, is to place the marinated or dry-rub strips on paper toweling and pat dry.

One of the simplest drying methods for the home jerky maker to use is drying in a kitchen oven with the door propped open slightly. Shown here are jerky strips on Hi Mountain jerky racks.

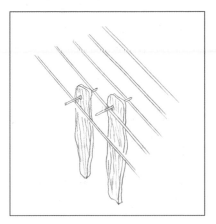

Jerky strips can also be suspended on ordinary oven racks using toothpicks threaded through holes in the ends of the strips.

Electric smokers that will reach temperatures of at least 140°F are also good choices for drying jerky strips.

insert toothpicks in the ends of the meat strips and hang the strips from the oven racks. This works, but they also fall easily, especially when you're trying to move the racks in and out of the oven.

If using a smokehouse or smoker, Hi Mountain recommends experimenting. All home smokers are different in size, wall thickness, location (inside or outside), outside temperature, wind, heat source, and so forth. Hi Mountain recommends smoking the jerky at 200°F for 1½ to 2 hours with smoke on; however, if your smoker will not reach 200°F, leave the meat in longer. Do not smoke for more than 3 hours until you have tasted the first batch. Do not overcook, and do not oversmoke. Too much smoke can produce a bitter flavor.

If using a dehydrator, Hi Mountain recommends that you follow your dehydrator instructions. Again, jerky does not have to be cooked so hard that you can't chew it. Test it frequently.

A food dehydrator that will reach a temperature of 140°F is an excellent tool for dehydrating and drying jerky.

Modern
Ground Jerky

Although sliced jerky is the easiest to make, ground-meat jerky has become increasingly popular, not only with commercial jerky makers but with home jerky makers as well. Ground-meat jerky has several advantages. It's less chewy, and it can be made from lesser

Ground-meat jerky has become extremely popular. It's easy to do if you have a grinder, and it utilizes the less-choice cuts of meat.

cuts of meat, as well as the small pieces of meat trimmings from butchering. To use all your butchered meat effectively, you might like to make both sliced and ground-meat jerky. Ground-meat jerky does require a bit more effort, and you'll need a means of grinding and extruding or shaping the ground meat.

THE MEAT

As with any jerky making, it's important to carefully follow safe meat processing methods, even more so with ground meat, as pathogens can be spread throughout ground meat. Also, as with all types of jerky making, it's important to cut away all fat and as much sinew as possible, especially with venison. Venison fat turns rancid, and sinew makes even ground jerky tougher to chew. Because the meat used is often butcher trimmings from carving out other choice cuts, including meat from the legs with lots of sinew and flank steak

Make sure you follow safe meat-processing procedures with ground meat because it's more easily contaminated. Cut away all fat and sinew.

from the ribs with quite a bit of fat, it does take a bit more time and effort to ensure a good, lean meat for the jerky.

GRINDING

Regardless of whether you use a hand or powered grinder, the meat should be cut up into chunks or strips that will fit readily into the grinder opening or throat. For hand grinders, the smaller you cut the chunks or strips, the easier it is to grind. Make sure there are no bones in the meat to stop an electric grinder or damage the worm gear and grinding plate and blade. A bone will definitely stop a hand grinder, but it is less likely to cause damage. The meat should be 40°F or colder and free of gristle and sinew. Using the meat stomper, slowly feed the meat into the throat of the grinder head. Do not force the meat, and never use your fingers to push the meat into the head. Used properly, today's grinders are very safe, especially when compared to older versions like my granddad's big grinder with a

Before the meat can be ground, it should be cut into long strips or chunks that will fit down your grinder throat.

big, wide, open throat. The family joke, "Don't get your tie in there," was really a reminder to all users to be extremely careful.

Grind the meat through the coarse plate first. We prefer our jerky made from coarse ground. If you want a finer grind, turn off the motor, and unplug the grinder. Next, remove the coarse plate, and clean the head of any sinew, fat, and gristle that has accumulated during the first grind. Reassemble the unit with the fine plate, plug the grinder in, and regrind the meat. If the meat mashes instead of coming through the plate in strings, unplug the grinder, remove all the meat from the grinder and plate, reassemble and tighten the grinder ring, making sure it's tighter than it was before, and begin to grind the meat again. When you're through grinding, run some saltine crackers through the grinder to help clean it out, then unplug the grinder, and disassemble the head. Wash all parts in hot, soapy water, and thoroughly rinse in hot water. Allow parts

Grind the meat using a hand or powered grinder. The LEM meat grinder makes short work of the chore.

to dry completely. Spray parts with food-grade silicone to prevent rust and keep your grinder in like-new condition while stored.

THE CURE

Although you can simply dry the meat, adding cure and seasonings not only provides a better means of preservation, but it adds taste as well. As with sliced-muscle meat, you can make up your own recipes or use any number of commercially prepared mixes. Many of the recipes in the muscle-meat chapter can also be used for ground-meat jerky. The following are a couple of homemade ground-meat recipes that we enjoy. As with muscle-meat jerky, ground meat must also be weighed for proper curing.

Regardless of whether you're using a homemade or commercial recipe, make sure you weigh the ground meat and use the correct amount of cure and seasonings.

Burch Ground Meat Jerky

2 lb. ground venison

2 teaspoons Morton Tender Quick

1 teaspoon each garlic powder and onion powder

½ teaspoon each dried red pepper and ground black pepper, or
  to suit

¼ cup brown sugar

Mix all the cure and spices together. Place the meat in a glass or plastic container. Sprinkle a little of the spice over the meat, and mix well with your hands. Then, add more spice, and mix until you have all the meat well coated with the cure mix. An alternative method is to dissolve the cure and spices in ½ cup of cold water. Pour this over the meat and mix thoroughly. Place a cover over the dish or pan, and refrigerate overnight to allow the cure and seasonings to work into the meat. Extrude or roll the meat out onto the waxed side of freezer paper, a jerky rack, or dehydrator tray.

Curing and seasoning adds to the flavor and preservation. First mix the spices and curing agents together.

Next, spread the mixed cure and seasoning over the meat.

Thoroughly mix the meat and cure/seasonings together.

Burch Ground Meat Jerky 2

2 lb. ground venison

2 teaspoons Morton Sugar Cure (Plain)

1 tablespoon Worcestershire sauce

¼ teaspoon each black pepper, garlic powder, onion powder, Liquid Smoke

Another, less spicy ground meat jerky recipe is also a favorite. Again, mix the spices with a little water and then thoroughly incorporate into the meat using your hands. Extrude and dry as mentioned.

COMMERCIAL MIXES

A number of commercial cure and seasoning mixes are also available. The following are some of the mixes I've tested and liked.

Uncle Buck's Regular Jerky Seasoning and Cure

Up to 10 lb. meat

4 teaspoons seasoning per 1 1b. of meat

¼ teaspoon cure per 1 1b. of meat

1 oz. water per 1 1b. of meat

The package will do 10 pounds of meat. Mix 4 teaspoons of seasoning, ¼ teaspoon of cure, and 1 ounce of water for each pound of ground meat used. Mix thoroughly until the mixture becomes tacky. Using a Jerky Cannon, squeeze strips on to a jerky rack. Place jerky rack on a cookie sheet, and dry strips in an oven at 200°F for 75 minutes on each side. Or, squeeze strips onto the racks of a dehydrator and dry, following dehydrator directions. The finished product must be refrigerated.

Uncle Buck's Snack Sticks

Up to 5 lb. meat
4 teaspoons seasoning per 1 1b. of meat
¼ teaspoon cure per 1 1b. of meat
1 oz. water per 1 1b. of meat

Another great tasting jerky is made with the Uncle Buck's Snack Sticks Seasoning. Extruded out into round sticks, this is a great homemade Slim Jim. The packet will treat 5 pounds of meat. According to the instructions; "Dissolve 4½ teaspoons of seasoning, ¼ teaspoon of cure, and 1 ounce of water to mix with each pound of meat. Mix thoroughly until the mixture becomes tacky. Process using one of the following methods: Stuff into natural or collagen casings and smoke in smoker until internal temperature of meat reaches 165°F. Or make Slim Jims with a Jerky Cannon and shoot them onto a cookie sheet. Dry in an oven at 200°F for 75 minutes per side or until internal temperature of meat reaches 165°F. Finished product must be refrigerated."

Purchased cures and mixes, such as the Uncle Buck's Snack Stick mix, are also available for making ground-meat jerky.

The cure and seasonings are added to cold water.

The ingredients are mixed well, and then the cure and seasoning mix is poured over the ground meat and thoroughly mixed.

Eastman Outdoors Jerky Cure and Seasoning

5 lb. lean meat
1 oz. seasoning
1 oz. cure
1 cup cold water

Use the leanest meat possible. To each 5 pounds, add 1 ounce seasoning, 1 ounce cure, and 1 cup of ice-cold water. Mix in a non-metallic bowl for 5 minutes or until sticky. Cover the bowl, and refrigerate for at least 4 hours. Use the Eastman Outdoors Jerky Gun to extrude the meat into perfect strips or sticks. Package will do 5 pounds of ground meat.

Hi Mountain Jerky Cure and Seasoning

1 to 3 lb. meat
½ cup water per pound of meat
Cure and seasoning according to weight

Make 1 to 3 pounds at a time. Hi Mountain suggests you start with a small batch at first. Mix cure and seasoning according to

Hi Mountain has a wide line of cures and seasonings.

Mix the cure and seasonings together and pour the mixture over the meat.

Mix well, and allow to cure overnight in a non-metallic container in the refrigerator.

weight chart. Add ½ cup ice water per pound of meat. Mix meat, water, and seasoning thoroughly for approximately 5 minutes or until sticky.

SHAPING THE GROUND MEAT

Ground-meat jerky is commonly formed into thin strips or round sticks. You can shape the meat into a jerky product in a number of ways. One of the simplest methods is to place a ball of meat on a piece of waxed paper or the waxed side of a piece of freezer paper. Place another piece of waxed paper over the meat ball, and use a rolling pin or straight-sided drinking glass to roll the meat patty out to a uniform thickness of about ⅛ to ³⁄₁₆ inch. Peel back the top paper, and use a kitchen knife to slice the rolled-out patty into strips

Ground-meat jerky can be shaped into strips or sticks. Shown here are Slim Jim-style sticks.

Ground-meat jerky can be shaped into thin jerky-style strips quite easily with waxed paper or the waxed side of freezer paper. Flatten a ball of cured and seasoned meat onto a piece of waxed paper.

Place another piece of waxed paper over the meat, and use a rolling pin to roll the meat out flat to about a ⅛-inch thickness. Remove the top waxed paper piece.

Use a kitchen knife—not a sharp knife—to separate the meat into thin strips. The meat strips can be flipped over onto a dehydrator tray for drying.

about 1 inch wide. Take care not to slice through the bottom piece of waxed paper. Line a jerky rack or cookie cooling rack with freezer paper with the waxed side up. Transfer the strips to the jerky rack by flipping the waxed paper over onto the freezer paper and peeling the waxed paper from the back side. If using the freezer paper, dry the strips until the surface is sealed, flip this over onto a drying rack, and peel off the freezer paper. This gives the ground meat strips a little stability for each of the handling steps. When completely dry, tear or break apart the strips on the cut lines. The strips can also be flipped onto a dehydrator rack for drying.

Another method of creating the strips from ground meat is to line a sheet-cake or other baking pan with plastic wrap. Press the ground meat into the pan to a suitable thickness. Partially freeze the pan, remove meat from the pan, peel off the plastic wrap, and slice into strips. The partially frozen meat is much easier to work with and slice.

Extruding ground meat through a hand-held, ground-jerky-meat extruder is a very common and popular method. These tools

A jerky extruder, such as the Hi Mountain Jerky Gun, can also be used to shape the meat. These normally come with two tips: one for strips and one for sticks.

resemble caulking guns, and most come with interchangeable tips—both a flat tip for jerky strips and a round tip for stick jerky.

With the meat ground and cured, wet your clean hands in cold water, then take about a cup of the ground meat and roll it between your hands to form into a roll small enough to slide down into the barrel of the jerky gun. Make sure the roll is wet enough to easily slide down into the barrel. Add more rolls until the barrel is full. Gently push the plunger down into the barrel, making sure to properly align the plastic plunger tip with the barrel so you don't damage the tip. Spray a jerky screen, such as the one from Hi Mountain, with a light coating of cooking oil. Pull the trigger gently to squeeze the strips or sticks onto the Jerky Screen, or extrude the sticks or strips out onto jerky racks lined with freezer paper following the directions above. Now you're ready to dry the jerky.

With wet hands, roll the cured and seasoned ground meat into thin rolls that will slide easily down into the jerky extruder.

Continue filling the tube.

Gently squeeze the handle to extrude the ground meat onto a jerky screen, such as that from Hi-Mountain.

The resulting extruded ground-meat jerky ready to dry.

The ultimate extruder is the LEM Patty and Jerky Machine, an accessory that fits onto the LEM Grinder. The unit allows you to grind and then extrude large quantities of ground patties or jerky in either strips or sticks, depending on the plate chosen. The accessory extrudes four sticks or strips at a time. The Jerky Machine comes with a special extruding plate; a holder for a roll of waxed butcher paper; one roll of waxed butcher paper; and a pair of stainless-steel scissors. If you grind meat only one time, assemble the jerky machine head, and attach it to the grinder before you start grinding. If you grind twice, attach the machine head before the second grind and use the extruding plate. The first step is to select the appropriate extruding plate, either the patty, jerky strip, or snack stick plate. Fasten to the front of the unit with the stainless steel screws.

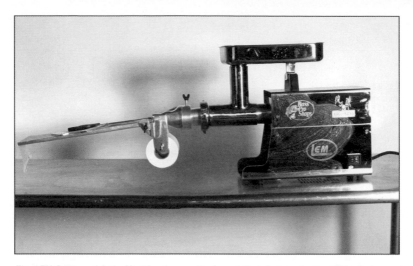

The LEM Patty and Jerky Machine is an attachment that fastens to the LEM grinder and extrudes sticks or strips of ground-meat jerky. You can grind and extrude at the same time or grind, mix, and extrude.

Remove the retaining ring from the grinder. Attach the grinder adapter to the grinder using the retaining ring, as you would a stuffing tube. Mount the jerky machine head to the adapter and secure it with the winged bolts. Place the meat chute in position, and secure it with the winged bolts. Attach the waxed paper roll to the jerky machine head using the paper rod and winged nuts. Thread the paper between the jerky machine head and the meat chute. Make sure the paper unrolls counter-clockwise from the back of the roll to place the waxed side up onto the chute. Pull the paper down the meat chute about 3 inches. Start grinding or extruding. The extruded material will push the paper down the meat chute. When the meat reaches the end of the chute, stop the grinder. Use the stainless steel scissors to cut the strips and waxed paper to the desired length and slide them off onto cookie sheets.

We found it better to grind, then extrude. As you grind, the meat is forced out onto waxed paper.

When the sticks are the length needed, cut the paper and sticks with the stainless-steel scissors.

The resulting jerky snack sticks on waxed paper and in pans, ready to dry.

DRYING

Ground-meat jerky can be dried using an oven, dehydrator, or smoker capable of reaching at least 200°F. Disease-causing micro-organisms are more difficult to eliminate in ground meat than whole meat strips. Be sure to follow the dehydrator manufacturer's directions when heating the product at the end of the drying time. An internal temperature of 160°F is necessary to eliminate disease-causing bacteria such as E. coli 0157:H7, if present.

If drying in an oven, place the strips or sticks on jerky racks, positioned over cookie sheets to catch drips. We have also used cookie cooling racks as jerky racks. Preheat oven to 200°F and, with

Ground-meat jerky can be dried in an oven set at 200°F. Make sure the meat attains an internal temperature of 160°F.

If using a dehydrator to dry the meat, follow the manufacturer's instructions. Shown here is a section of waxed-paper-shaped ground-meat jerky, ready for the dehydrator.

the oven door slightly open, heat for 1 to 2 hours or until the strips crack but do not break when bent. Increase heat to 275°F until internal temperature reaches 160°F. Ground-meat jerky strips tend to stick a bit more than muscle-meat strips. It's a good idea to turn the strips over to ensure even cooking and to prevent sticking. If using a dehydrator, make sure you follow the manufacturer's directions on drying jerky.

CHAPTER 7

More Jerky Recipes

The following jerky recipes can be used for lean beef, venison, or most other domestic or wild game. One especially good cut of beef for making jerky is a trimmed brisket. Another is beef chuck roast.

Lean beef makes some of the best jerky. As with any other meat used for jerky, use only the healthiest animals.

If purchasing meat cuts from the butcher for jerky, brisket is a great choice for sliced jerky.

To extend the use of ground meat for jerky, freeze in pre-weighed bags, such as the 1-pound bags shown. Then, make jerky as you need it by removing from the freezer the number of bags needed to fill your oven or dehydrator.

No matter what cut you use, consider freezing weighed amounts of ground meat, such as 1-pound packages, ahead of time. Then, you can take the exact amount you need from the freezer and prepare jerky on-demand throughout the year. Our nephew, Morgan, utilizes this method. Morgan started preparing his venison this way because he didn't have a grinder and had to get his deer meat ground at the butcher shop all at one time. Needless to say, a whole deer or two was way too much ground meat to prepare into jerky immediately. Therefore, he froze the meat and made jerky as needed, always having a fresh batch. Morgan now has his favorite recipe down to a science. His round dehydrator will hold 5 pounds of meat and dries in 6 hours.

Drying, as mentioned in previous chapters, may be done in a kitchen oven, dehydrator, or smoker.

Morgan's Jerky

1 lb. ground venison (fresh or frozen)
1 tablespoon Morton Tender Quick
¼ teaspoon black pepper
½ teaspoon onion powder
¼ teaspoon garlic powder
¼ teaspoon Worcestershire sauce
1 to 2 teaspoons crushed red pepper (or to suit)
Liquid Smoke

The above amounts are for 1 pound of ground venison. For each 5-pound batch, Morgan adds three tablespoons crushed red pepper. The Liquid Smoke isn't added to the ground meat. Instead, it is sprayed on during the drying process. Morgan dries the batch long enough to set the top side, then sprays that side with Liquid Smoke. Halfway through the drying process, he turns the strips over on the dehydrator trays and sprays the other sides. He says the Liquid Smoke isn't lost in the ground meat mixture with this method and has a fresher, smoked flavor. You can also brush on Liquid Smoke with a pastry brush.

Gingered Jerky

2 lb. lean meat, thinly sliced
1 tablespoon freshly ground ginger root or 1 ½ teaspoon ground
    ginger
2 tablespoons salt or Morton Tender Quick
1 teaspoon powdered garlic
1 teaspoon onion powder
½ cup brown sugar

If you like the slightly hot taste of ginger, you may enjoy this type of jerky. Thoroughly mix the dry ingredients, and then coat the meat strips with the mix. Place in a non-metallic container or sealable plastic bag, and refrigerate overnight for 10 hours. Rinse, pat dry between layers of paper towels, and dehydrate or oven dry.

Whiskey Pepper Jerky

2 lb. lean venison or beef, thinly sliced
1 cup whiskey or bourbon
1 teaspoon freshly ground coarse black pepper
1 tablespoon salt or Morton Tender Quick
½ cup soy sauce
½ cup water
2 cloves minced garlic
2 tablespoons Worcestershire sauce

You can achieve a different, Western-style flavoring with the addition of whiskey or bourbon and fresh, coarse-ground black pepper. Stir all ingredients together. Place the meat strips in a

Always use a covered plastic or glass container when marinating meat strips. Plastic wrap can be used for the cover. Sealable plastic bags can also be used for marinating.

non-metallic container, and then pour marinade over and mix the strips. Marinate in the refrigerator overnight for 10 hours. Drain, pat dry between layers of paper towels, and dehydrate or oven dry.

Teriyaki Venison Jerky

2 lb. lean venison, thinly sliced
2 tablespoons Morton Tender Quick
½ cup teriyaki sauce or marinade
1 cup pineapple juice
½ cup soy sauce
1 teaspoon smoke flavoring
1 teaspoon black pepper

We love deer loin steaks cooked on the grill and like to marinate them with teriyaki sauce for a couple of hours before cooking. Doing so adds flavor and makes the steaks even more tender. Teriyaki sauce can also impart flavor to venison or other meat jerky.

Soak the strips in the marinade overnight in a refrigerator, and then drain, pat dry between layers of paper towels, and dehydrate or oven dry.

Hot and Spicy Szechwan Jerky

1 lb. ground venison
1 tablespoon Morton Tender Quick
1 package hot and spicy Szechwan seasoning mix (¾ oz.)
1 tablespoon soy sauce (or to suit)

This is another quick-to-make jerky because you can buy the spice mix at the store, and little mixing is required. Simply add the Szechwan seasoning packet and Tender Quick to the ground meat and mix well. Then, sprinkle the soy sauce over the meat and blend. Extrude into the desired shape, and dry in oven or dehydrator.

A package of hot and spicy Szechwan seasoning mix, used to flavor oriental dishes, makes flavorful jerky. Sprinkle the mix over a flattened patty of ground venison. Fold over to knead in the spices, much like kneading bread dough.

Sprinkle on the desired amount of soy sauce, and knead in as well.

One method of preparing ground meat for jerky is to press the mixture into a dish lined with plastic wrap. Place the dish in the freezer until partially frozen.

Pull from the pan, and slice the partially frozen meat into strips or sticks so that they're ready to dehydrate.

Note: Other store-bought seasoning mixes, such as sweet and sour, also make tasty flavored jerky.

Chili Sticks

1 lb. ground venison
1 tablespoon Morton Tender Quick
2 teaspoons chili powder
½ teaspoon garlic powder
½ teaspoon onion powder
½ teaspoon ground red pepper (or to suit)

This is an easy, flavorful jerky that is best made into snack sticks. Mix together the dry spices. Pat the ground meat into a flat shape, sprinkle on the spice mixture, and work in by folding over, adding more spice, and folding over again until all the spice is well blended into the ground meat. This recipe makes a very mild chili.

Chili-flavored jerky is another quick ground-meat recipe. Mix the desired spices, adding chili powder and red pepper to taste.

Knead the spices into the ground meat.

Another method of preparing a ground meat mixture is to simply pat the mixture into a ¾-inch-thick slab on a piece of plastic wrap. Place the cutting board and all in the freezer to partially freeze, then remove, slice into strips or sticks, and dry.

If you prefer a spicier version, increase chili powder and ground red pepper to suit. Extrude into the shape desired, and dry in oven or dehydrator.

Easy-Does-It Oven Jerky

2 lb. venison steak, sliced into thin strips
Morton Sugar Cure (plain)
Steak sauce, barbecue sauce, Liquid Smoke, or other flavored
**   sauce such as sweet and sour sauce.**

This is one of the simplest recipes and a great choice for the beginning jerky maker. Simply rub the Morton Sugar Cure onto all sides of the slices, and place on racks in an oven with the door open slightly. Set oven at 200°F, and dry until the internal temperature reaches 165°F. When the jerky is almost dry, remove and brush your favorite steak sauce onto the strips. Barbecue sauce, flavored marinade, or Liquid Smoke can also be brushed onto the strips. Sweet and sour sauce is especially good. If using Liquid Smoke, only brush on one side of the strips, as it can quickly become too strong. Return to the oven until the jerky is dry and the steak sauce coating is well set.

BBQ Grilled Jerky

Meat, thinly sliced
1 gallon water
1 cup canning or pickling salt
Brown sugar
Curry powder
Wood chips (apple, hickory, or mesquite)

BBQ jerky is made by brining the sliced meat in a mixture of canning salt and water. Stir the brine until salt is dissolved, and then add the meat strips.

Mix 1 cup canning or pickling salt with 1 gallon of water. Place the strips in the brine, and refrigerate overnight. Remove from the brine, wash in cold water, and pat dry. Sprinkle all sides of the meat strips with brown sugar. Place the meat strips on a jerky rack or cookie sheet, and coat with a light dusting of curry powder. Bake in a hot oven for 15 to 20 minutes. Switch the trays around two to three times during the baking, especially if the oven is full. In the meantime, soak wood chips—apple, hickory, or mesquite—for 30 to 40 minutes. Place started charcoal on one side or one corner of the grill, or start after placing and add the smoking chips. Remove the meat from the oven and place on a wire rack on the opposite side or corner of the grill. With the lid closed, but vents open, smoke for 2 to 3 hours, testing for doneness in about 3 hours.

Hot Brined Marinade

1 cup canning or pickling salt
1 cup vinegar

Boiling in a brine solution is one method of being sure your jerky is thoroughly cooked. Drain and pat dry; then, dry in the oven or dehydrator.

1 cup brown sugar

4 cups water

One method of heating muscle-meat jerky for safety is to use a hot brine. Above is a recipe for a very basic hot brine. Add seasonings such as black pepper, red pepper, onion, and/or garlic to taste. Mix the brine ingredients in a stainless-steel pan, bring the brine to a boil, and place the sliced strips into the boiling brine. Leave in just a few minutes or until the meat changes color. Remove from the brine and pat dry. The strips are now ready to be dried into jerky in the oven or dehydrator.

Biltong (South African Beef Jerky)

For almost 400 years, biltong has been a favorite with South Africans and Zimbabweans. The word is derived from two Dutch

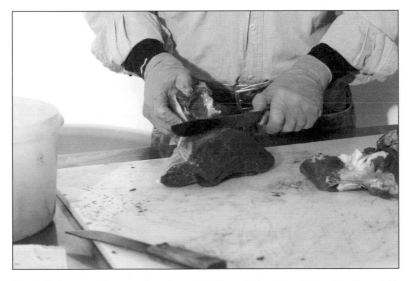

The buttock or rump is a common cut used in Biltong. Clean fat and sinew from the outside of the meat before slicing.

words: "bil" referring to buttock and "tong" referring a strip. This is an air-dried, salted, and mildly spiced meat commonly made from the buttocks or rumps of a beef or buffalo. Rump roasts, eye of round, or Porterhouse roasts are the most common cuts of meat, although in Africa the best cuts are called silverside (buttocks or rumps) and topside. Other game meat, including ostrich, is also used. A more pungent version, called Tassal, was made in France during the Middle Ages, in Batavia, and later by the Dutch in South Africa. Beer and biltong is still a popular combination in South Africa. Biltong was and is also used in other ways—thinly sliced or shredded for a filling for omelets, pancakes, and crepes. It's also used in salads and as spreads. A South African favorite is a slice of biltong on freshly baked bread lathered with butter.

As you can guess, many biltong recipes have been passed down through the generations. Two basic methods can be used to make them. In both, vinegar is employed to make the meat more tender as well as to add flavor. The vinegar also provides a dark, shiny appearance to the dried meat.

After slicing, be sure to check the slices and trim any unwanted fat or sinew.

Seasoned Biltong

2 cups pickling or canning salt
½ cup brown sugar
4 teaspoons bicarbonate of soda
1 ½ teaspoons black pepper
Seasonings to suit

In the first method, the meat strips are dipped in vinegar. Any vinegar will work—white or cider. The seasoning mix is applied to the strips, and they are refrigerated overnight to allow the vinegar and seasonings to work. The seasoning mix contains the staples of salt, sugar, and black pepper. Bicarbonate of soda helps tenderize the sliced meat. Other seasonings such as onion, garlic powder, or ground red pepper can be added, but ground coriander is the traditional addition.

Marinated Biltong

1 cup white vinegar
1 cup of brown malt vinegar
1 tablespoon of brown sugar
½ teaspoon coarse ground coriander

In the second method, the meat is laid out on a smooth surface and sprinkled with white pepper and pickling or canning salt. Make sure to coat all parts of the meat, turning as needed. Make up a marinade by stirring the sugar and spices into the vinegar. Mix enough marinade using the above proportions to cover the sliced meat. Next, place the meat strips in a large sealable plastic bag or glass or plastic container, and refrigerate for 24 hours. If using a sealable bag, occasionally turn the bag to help coat all parts of the meat strips. Remove the strips, and dry them by placing them between paper towels and patting dry.

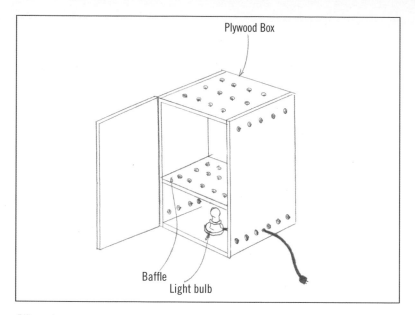

Biltong dryer.

The typical method of drying biltong was to hang it in a breezy place out of direct sunlight but not in deep shade. (It must also be protected from varmints and vermin.) As with any jerky, it should be dried to your personal taste. It should be hard and dark on the outside but red and with just a little bit of moistness on the inside. You can of course dry biltong as any other jerky recipe, in an oven or dehydrator.

Home biltong makers often made their own dryers from a cardboard or wooden box. Cut or drill ventilation holes in the sides near the bottom and in the top. Fit ⅜-inch wooden dowels in holes near the top of the box to hold the biltong strips. Place a 60- to 75-watt light bulb inside the box. If making a wooden box, adding a baffle with holes in it will provide more even heat and prevent drippings from contacting the light bulb.

CHAPTER **8**

Small Game and Wildfowl Jerky

Upland gamebirds, waterfowl, and small game can all be made into jerky. The type of jerky—muscle meat or ground meat—depends on the species being used. Small game such as rabbits, squirrels, groundhog, and others, as well as ducks and geese, are best

Geese, ducks, and small game can all be made into excellent jerky.

made into ground-meat recipes. Small game often don't provide large enough cuts of meat for slices. The dark meat of ducks and geese, especially snow geese, usually tastes better when ground with other, milder meats or when made into a spicy ground-meat recipe. In fact, a great way of cleaning out your freezer is to make up a smorgasbord of ground-meat jerky from whatever overabundance of game meat you have on hand at the end of the season.

Ground-Meat Smorgasbord Jerky

2 lb. wild game meat, ground
2 tablespoons Morton Tender Quick
1 teaspoon lemon pepper
1 teaspoon onion powder
1 teaspoon garlic powder
1 tablespoon soy sauce
½ cup water
3 to 4 drops hot sauce (or more if you prefer more heat)

As with all other types of meat, make sure you use safe field dressing and butchering processes, especially when making ground-meat jerky. Pathogens can easily be spread throughout the ground meat. Also, make sure you use meat only from healthy animals. Debone all the meat from the game animals or birds, and remove all fat and gristle. Cut away all bloody meat, and remove any shot from gunshot game. Ground-meat smorgasbord jerky is a case where you can use even the tougher, lesser cuts, including the thighs of birds such as wild turkeys or geese. If you use the legs, make sure you remove all the tiny, flexible tendons and bones. It's a good idea to first soak all the deboned pieces in salt water overnight in a refrigerator. This will help remove some of the gaminess and also tenderize some of the tougher pieces. If the meat hasn't been frozen, freeze it for 60 days. Partially thaw the meat, then grind it.

The first step is to debone the birds and small game. Then, grind the meat. Add the cure and seasoning, refrigerate, and dry.

Mix the ingredients together, making sure the spices are dissolved in the liquid. Pour the seasoning and cure over the ground meat in a non-metallic bowl, and mix well until tacky. Refrigerate overnight, extrude or form, and then dry. This seasoned and cured ground meat can be made into an excellent snack stick.

TURKEY JERKY

Domestic and wild turkeys are large enough to be made into jerky in the sliced-muscle meat method. Only the breast meat is

Turkey breast, both wild and domestic, can be made into a mouth-watering muscle-meat jerky.

used for this procedure. As with other types of muscle-meat jerky, remove all fat and connective tissue. Also, remove the skin. Then, slice into ¼-inch-thick strips. Partially freezing to firm the meat will help with slicing it into uniform, thin strips. Some of the best jerky I've tasted is the Hi Mountain Turkey Hunter's Bourbon Blend Jerky Cure and Seasoning. After cutting the meat into strips, weigh the meat so you know the exact amount of cure and seasoning mix needed. Mix the spices, and cure according to the mixing chart (per weight) included with the instructions. Mix only the amount needed. Be sure to store the remaining unmixed spices, and cure in an air-tight container until needed. Lay the strips flat on an even surface, and pat dry with a paper towel. Apply the mixed spices and cure to the prepared meat, using the sprinkler bottle included in

The Hi Mountain Turkey Hunter's Bourbon Blend Jerky Cure and Seasoning Mix creates a great-tasting, wild turkey jerky.

Debone the turkey breasts; remove skin, fat, and sinew; and then slice the meat into ¼-inch-thick strips.

Weigh the sliced strips.

Lay the strips on a flat surface, and sprinkle with the proper amount of cure and seasoning mix according to the weight of the turkey strips.

the package. Sprinkle the first side of meat with approximately half of the mixture. Next, turn the meat over, and sprinkle the remaining mixture on the meat. Put seasoned strips in a large mixing bowl, and tumble by hand until the mixture has been spread evenly on all sides of the meat. Stack the strips, pressed together tightly, in a non-metallic container or sealable plastic bag. Refrigerate for at least 24 hours. Hi Mountain Jerky Cure and Seasoning is formulated to penetrate the meat at the rate of $\frac{1}{4}$ inch per 24 hours; do not cure the meat any less than that. You're now ready to dry or dehydrate the jerky.

Mix the cure, seasonings, and weighed strips in a non-metallic bowl; cover; refrigerate overnight; and then dry or dehydrate.

Sliced-Meat Turkey Jerky

2 lb. wild turkey breast strips
2 teaspoons black pepper
1 teaspoon onion powder
1 teaspoon garlic powder
2 tablespoons Morton Tender Quick
4 tablespoons brown sugar
1 teaspoon Liquid Smoke
1 cup water or bourbon

You can also make up your own turkey-jerky cure and seasoning mix per the recipe above. Make sure cure, liquids, and seasonings are well mixed together. Pour the cure and seasoning mix over the strips, and then place the strips in a non-metallic container. Mix well, making sure all surfaces of the meat are well coated. Cover and refrigerate for 24 hours. Remove, pat dry, and dehydrate or dry.

DRYING

Small game jerky can be dried in a dehydrator following the manufacturer's instructions. It can also be dried in an oven set at 200°F. The ground-meat jerky can be dried with any of the methods mentioned throughout this book. The turkey jerky strips can be placed on wire racks or suspended in the oven. Make sure you have a pan below the jerky to catch drippings. It's also a good idea to spray racks with cooking oil to prevent sticking. Wild turkey meat

Perfectly dehydrated turkey jerky is not only great looking but makes great eating as well.

tends to dry quicker than red meat, so check the meat after about an hour's drying time. Properly dried jerky should bend but not break. Meat made from fowl must be heated to an internal temperature of 165°F to kill pathogens. There also tends to be more oil, especially in domestic turkey meat. This will bead up on the meat during the drying process. When the jerky is done, pat dry any oil from the surface. After jerky has dried completely, store in airtight containers in a dry, cool area. You can also freeze and/or vacuum pack turkey jerky for longer storage.

CHAPTER 9

Fish Jerky

Dried fish, in one form or another, has been a staple food of mankind for thousands of years. Whether living near fresh or saltwater sources, people have regularly dried a variety of fish as a way of preserving it for future meals. Native Americans on both

The Native Americans dried fish such as salmon split and hung it over wooden frameworks.

the East and West Coasts, for example, smoked and dried salmon for winter use. This smoked and dried meat would often keep until the next season. The eastern and western inhabitants also pounded the dried fish into a powder and traded it with the Native Americans of the Plains. Fish drying on racks in the traditional method is still seen in the coastal native villages of Alaska and Canada. Dried fish was also extremely important in Europe. In northern Europe, dried codfish is still a common food in many households.

THE MEAT

It's recommended to use only lean-meat fish, including freshwater fish such as bass, brook trout, crappies, bluegills, walleyes, and perch. If using freshwater fish, it's important to use only fish that are fresh and completely free of parasites. Good choices in ocean fish include flounder, codfish, and even cuts of tuna that are free of fat. Oilier fish and those with a high fat content, such as snapper, mackerel, mullet, whitefish, carp, catfish, and pike, are not suitable for making into fish jerky. The high oil and fat content makes the jerky prone to spoilage. In many of these fish, it's almost impossible to trim off the fat, as the fat is evenly distributed throughout the flesh. If these fish are smoked, however, they can often be used with good results. In fact, smoked fish such as salmon and trout, although not technically a jerky because it is not dried, has long been a staple for many cultures and is a real delicacy.

Fish can deteriorate and decompose rapidly in heat as well as from the enzymes found in the flesh of fish. This is the main reason fish jerky should only be made of freshly caught and killed fish. The fish can be kept on ice a short period of time until you can make jerky from them. Fish should be free of slime, and the flesh should be firm with a slight fishy smell. Clean and fillet the fish as soon as you can to assure freshness. Make sure the fillets are well cleaned in

Fish jerky or dried-salted fish has been a staple food source for many cultures. Fish with little oil or fat content, such as the largemouth bass shown here, are the best choices.

fresh, cold, running water to remove any blood. Cut the fillets into ¼-inch-thick strips from 4 to 6 inches long. Do not make the strips any thicker or they will be hard to dry. If using small fish, such as bluegill, you may not need to cut the fillets into smaller strips.

To thoroughly kill any parasites present in fish, freeze the fish for at least 48 hours before curing or freeze the jerky after dehydrating.

CURING

Many types of fish used for jerky are commonly salt cured before dehydrating. This salt cure can be a dry or a liquid variety. Homemade cures can be used, or a number of cures are also available in retail stores. The following are two traditional methods. For a brine cure, use ¼ cup of fine pickling or canning salt to 2 cups of water. If this volume doesn't cover the fish, prepare more brine following the same proportions of salt and water. This amount will brine 1 to 2 pounds of fish strips. Make sure the salt is thoroughly dissolved in the water, and then pour the brine over the strips. Use a glass container, cover, and place in the refrigerator for 48 hours. This salt curing not only draws out the moisture from the flesh, but it also aids in preservation and concentrates the amino acids.

You can also use a dry brine, allowing the dry salt to work into the meat and bring out the moisture. Place a thin layer of salt in a glass pan or dish. Apply a coating of salt to each fish strip and place in the pan. Layer the strips in the pan, making sure all strips are well coated with the salt. Cover the dish with plastic food wrap or a tight lid and place in a refrigerator for 48 hours.

In either case, remove the strips from the curing container, rinse under cold water, and pat dry. Now you're ready to dry or dehydrate. Simple salting and drying doesn't produce a very tasty

Canning or pickling salt is used to cure the fish into jerky.

The fish must be filleted and then cut into strips about ¼-inch thick and 5 inches long. Panfish fillets can often be used whole. Pat the strips dry.

fish jerky. To add taste, lightly coat the strips on both sides with soy sauce, Liquid Smoke, or Worcestershire sauce before drying.

Fish Seasoning Mix

½ **cup brown sugar**
½ **cup salt**
1 **teaspoon garlic powder**
1 **teaspoon onion powder**
2 **teaspoons white pepper**

You can also make a seasoning mix to add flavor to the fish strips. Above is a typical mix. Mix together and allow the mix to set overnight in an airtight container to blend the flavors. A pinch of powdered red pepper (or to suit) can be added to the mix if a hotter jerky is desired. Remove the strips from the original brine,

Although salt alone will cure the meat, adding brown sugar, spices, and other flavorings adds to the taste.

Make sure salt, sugar, and spices are well mixed.

Spread the cure and seasoning mixture over the fish strips, making sure they are all well covered.

Place a layer of the cure and seasoning mixture in the bottom of a non-metallic bowl or pan, and layer the treated strips in place, adding additional cure and seasoning mix as needed. Cover and allow to cure in a refrigerator overnight.

rinse off the brine or salt, and pat dry. Coat the strips with the mix, and allow them to sit in the refrigerator for about 2 hours. Dry or dehydrate.

Cured Salmon

Fresh salmon
½ cup white sugar
½ cup brown sugar
1 gallon cold water
1 ¾ cups of Morton Tender Quick mix or Morton Sugar Cure (Plain) mix.

An excellent cured salmon recipe comes from Morton Salt. Clean and eviscerate salmon. Remove head, fins, tail, and ½ inch from each side along the belly incision. For salmon weighing less than 10 pounds, cut into 3-inch steaks. Split steaks along the backbone, leaving skin on if desired. If salmon is greater than 10 pounds, cut into 1½-inch steaks.

Prepare 1 gallon of brine for each 5 pounds of salmon using proportions of water, sugar, brown sugar, and Morton Tender Quick or Morton Sugar Cure (Plain) mix as listed. Completely submerge the salmon in brine, using a ceramic plate or bowl to weigh down the fish and keep it submerged. Cure in refrigerator for 16 hours. Remove salmon, and rinse it in cool water. Pat dry and cook as desired.

Salmon may also be smoked in an electric smoker, following the manufacturer's instructions. The salmon must be heated to an internal temperature of 160°F and held at this temperature for at least 30 minutes. Refrigerate if not consumed immediately.

DRYING

In the past, fish was simply dried outside. Typically, the Native Americans split the salmon carcasses and hung them over wooden frameworks in the shade but in an area with good air circulation and quite often with a smoky fire beneath. You can also dry fish outside, given the right circumstances, but make sure it is well covered to keep away insects. A smoky fire can be helpful not only in the drying but in keeping insects away. Fish can be easily dried in a dehydrator by following the manufacturer's instructions. Fish jerky can also be dried in an oven. Place on wire racks over cookie sheets to catch the drippings. Set the oven at 150°F and with the oven door slightly open. Dry for about an hour. Then, turn the strips over and dry for another hour. Test the jerky strips. The finished jerky should be like red-meat jerky. You should be able to bend it without breaking. It should not be crumbly or crunchy. When dried properly, there

Wash off salt and seasonings and dry in an oven or dehydrator until the internal temperature of the jerky strips is 160°F.

should be no moisture on the surface of the jerky sticks. For safety, the internal temperature must reach 160°F.

STORAGE

Properly cured and dried, fish jerky should last for a long time in sealed containers in a cool, dry place. For safety, you may prefer to freeze and/or vacuum pack the jerky strips. Storing the prepared jerky in the freezer will also take care of any parasites.

Smoked Salmon

Fresh salmon
Hi Mountain Alaskan Salmon Brine Mix
1 gallon ice water

Although not an actual jerky, smoked salmon is easy to make with the Hi Mountain Alaskan Salmon Brine Mix. The brine mix is made with pure maple sugar. The package contains two bags of mix. Dissolve one packet in 1 gallon of ice water. The fish should be fresh and well chilled before curing. Immerse the fish in the brine solution, making sure it is well covered. Place it in a refrigerator for 24 hours. Remove the fish from the brine, rinse it well with fresh, cold water, and pat it dry. Let the fish sit at room temperature for about 30 minutes and then smoke it. Smoking time can vary depending on the type of smoker, location, outside temperature, and so forth. The fish should be smoked until the internal temperature reaches 160°F. If you cannot get fish to the desired internal temperature with your smoker, place it in the oven to finish once the desired color is reached.

Sources

Bradley Smokers, 800-665-4188, www.bradleysmoker.com

Cabelas, www.cabelas.com

Cajun Injector, www.cajuninjector.com

Center for Disease Control and Prevention, National Center for Infectious Diseases, Division of Parasitic Diseases, www.cdc.gov/foodsafety

Chef'sChoice, EdgeCraft Corp., 800-342-3255, www.chefschoice.com

Chronic Wasting Disease, www.CWD-info.org

Eastman Outdoors, 800-241-4833, www.eastmanoutdoors.com

Excalibur, 800-875-4254, www.excaliburdehydrator.com

Hi Mountain Jerky, 800-829-2285, www.himtnjerky.com

Lansky Sharpeners, 800-825-2675, www.lanskysharpeners.com

Lawry's Foods, 800-9-LAWRYS, www.lawrys.com

LEM Products, 877-536-7763, www.lemproducts.com

Morton Salt, 800-725-8847, www.mortonsalt.com

National Center for Home Food Preservation, www.uga.edu/nchfp

Open Country and Garden Master Dehydrators, Nesco/American Harvest, 800-288-4545, www.nesco.com or www.opencountryc- ampware.com

Sun-Bird Seasoning Mix, Williams Foods, Inc., www.williamsfoods .com

USDA, Food Safety and Inspection Service, www.fsis.usda.gov

The Wildlife Management Institute, www.wildlifemanagementinsti- tute.org